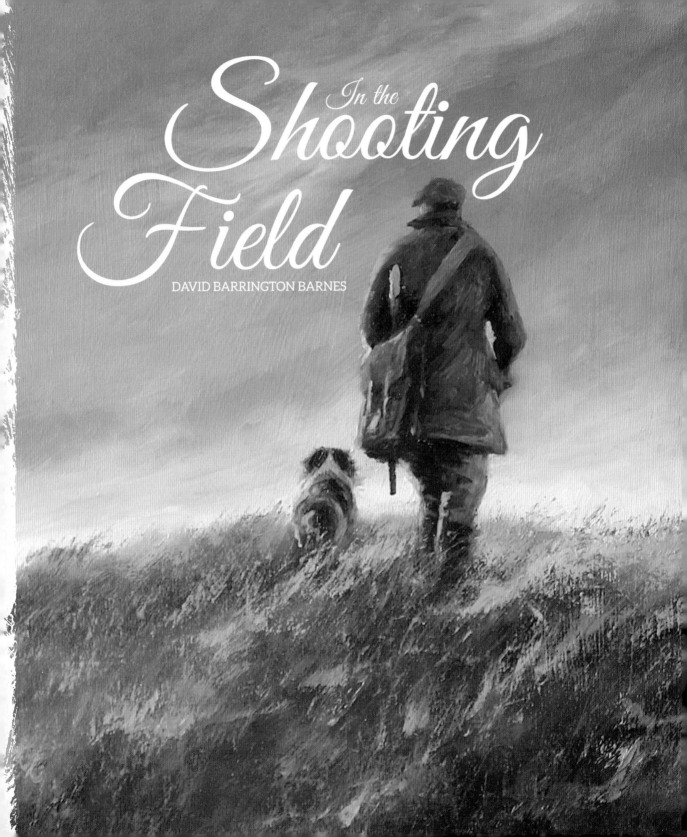

In the Shooting Field

Field

DAVID BARRINGTON BARNES

Master Eagerness & Uncle Experience

TO MY SON, TOBY,
With whom I share a passion for the shooting sports.

"There is a passion for hunting something deeply implanted in the human breast."

Charles Dickens.

AUTHOR
David Barrington Barnes

EDITOR
Peter Carr

DEPUTY EDITOR
Nicola Turner

DESIGN
Chris Sweeney

COVER IMAGE
Mick Cawston / Sally Mitchell Fine Arts

PHOTOGRAPHY
Photographs supplied by the author, James Marchington and Becky Sealey

ISBN 978-0-9549597-7-7

Printed in Europe by Cliffe Enterprise Print Partnership
ChinaPrintingService.com (Beijing Tiantu Printing Co., Ltd.)
Huatong Building A, Office 801,19 Chegongzhuang West Road.
Haidian District, Beijing, China

Blaze Publishing Ltd
Lawrence House, Morell Street, Leamington Spa,
Warwickshire, CV32 5SZ
Tel: +44 (0) 1926 339 808
Fax: +44 (0) 1926 470 400
Email: info@blazepublishing.co.uk
Website: www.blazepublishing.co.uk

Foreword

First I must say, David Barrington Barnes, DBB or, as most of us know him, "The Boy Barrington", is a true sporting gent of the old school. I have worked with him for years on *Sporting Rifle* and *Modern Gamekeeping* magazines, where he has never failed to deliver his honest, informative, and often compelling copy. But well before that I knew him as a regular scribe in various sporting journals, where his jottings have always retained my attention, and often made me laugh out loud. This, his latest book, is so much more than a collection of anecdotes. It is a rare seam of candid sporting excellence, gauged not by numbers in the game bag, or marksmanship alone, but by a gentleman's perspective of sport enjoyed in the shooting field.

DBB is a rarity today in that he is a true all-round field sportsman, (indeed I cannot wait for his third tome *On The Banks of Loch and Stream*). David derives the same pleasure from feeling the rod bend when he hooks into a fish, as he does when engaging a high, fast curling pheasant, or a downwind goose coming at him like a Lancaster bomber on a strafing run, or outwitting that wily roebuck he has earmarked for the larder. DBB retells his exploits in the humble way that only he can. His trials and tribulations are covered with the same eagerness and detail as those rare red letter days when Diana delivers game in abundance, when one is on form and the shooting arm swings true. His enthusiasm is as bright today on the best of formal driven days, as it was over half a century ago, when as a small boy he first followed the call of Nimrod, armed with nought but a diminutive garden gun in pursuit of rats.

This book covers an absolute wealth of subjects concerning the pursuit of game with the shotgun, and mostly with a much-loved but often silently chagrined fido for company. The author obviously believes that sharing sport with a canine companion greatly enhances the experience. DBB's recounting of his gun dog exploits will win a smile and occasional chuckle out of the hardest of dog handlers reading these pages. Most who work gundogs will relate to his angst and occasional euphoria – relative of course to their particular four legged delinquencies and achievements recorded here.

From ferreting rabbits, to days at that prince of gamebirds, the red grouse, and all else in between, DBB covers every aspect of their pursuit from his own perspective.

David has always been willing to lend a hand, or share his wisdom with a fellow sportsman if asked, and is ever keen to introduce youngsters to the sport. It is an absolute pleasure to write this foreword for his latest book that follows hot on the heels of *On The Deer Path*. He has a rare skill with the pen, and I feel privileged to count him as a friend.

Peter Carr Editor: *Modern Gamekeeping*
Duddon Valley, February 2014

Introduction

When I published my deerstalking memoir *On The Deer Path*, I was delighted by how favourably it was received. It was the subject of several enthusiastic and approving reviews. In addition, the individual comments of my fellow deerstalkers demonstrated that my reminiscences in the field and woods had hit the spot. Such general approval was all very gratifying.

The only criticism that *On The Deer Path* provoked was that I must have been an obsessive deerstalker to expend so much time and effort on the pursuit of deer. These critics suggested that my interest in deer was over the top, and that mine was a life lacking balance.

In The Shooting Field is my answer to them. The exploits recounted in it show that for over 50 years I have also been an enthusiastic rough and game shooter, and amateur gamekeeper. I have been a shooting man for far longer than a deerstalker. Since becoming involved in deer stalking I have carried on all my shooting pursuits - rough and game shooting - with undiminished enthusiasm. So I hope this book proves that I have shared my passion for low ground deerstalking with my love of shooting.

In The Shooting Field is a celebration of my life and times as a shooting man. I very much hope my shooting, but not deerstalking, friends who had the patience to read *On The Deer Path* will share with me the enjoyable, amusing and exciting days in the field that I describe.

A deerstalker reader of *On The Deer Path* described it as a book to read and then revisit from time to time in front of a log fire with a glass of whisky at hand. If a shooting reader is of the same opinion about *In The Shooting Field,* then I will have met the modest aspirations I had in writing the book: to share the pleasure I

have had and to give enjoyment to the shooting man.

David Barrington Barnes
Suffolk, January 2014

Contents

Princely Shooting, Perfect Shots

Most of us are capable of pulling off the perfect shot on occasion. There will be an unfortunate few, and I count myself among their ranks, that will need a knowledgeable expert on gun fit, and maybe a lesson or two, to set them on the right path. However, if you have the heart of the hunter, princely shooting is not an unattainable nirvana. Lady Luck is often a required element of course, but with even moderate shooting skills a perfect shot or two will certainly come your way most seasons. And when it does, it is these special moments that will live long in the memory. They are far more important than a full game cart or swelling game bag.

This first chapter of jottings sets the scene for the book proper: it catalyses my joy to be out in the shooting field, and celebrates those perfect shot memories that have made a lifetime of early rises, far travel, and inclement conditions, all worth it. When it is my time to ascend Valhalla, I'm sure these remarkable shots will be as vivid then as they were on the day of achievement, and for those young guns just starting out, I hope they motivate you to shoot on, if of course any additional incentive was ever needed.

The Golden Ball is the large field that lies on the north-eastern boundary of my fen shoot. One afternoon, I was working my dog along the boundary dyke. I was, at that time, on my own as my two companions had already taken a dyke towards the middle of the shoot and were at work, with their dogs, three or four hundred yards upwind of me. While my spaniel was hunting the boundary dyke on my immediate right, I was keeping an eye on the distant figures of my friends in the hope that they might flush a bird. If they did, it was likely to roll over and come back down their dyke to me rather than fly into the stiff breeze.

That is just what happened. I saw a pheasant – it was a hen bird – flush from the dyke and curl in my direction. As she caught the wind, she flew higher and higher until she was high above the flat fen field from which I watched her. She was coming downwind so high and fast she gave the impression of being out of shot. I had ample time to watch her as she came on towards me.

In the end, I picked a moment and upped my gun, swinging though her as fast as I could. To my complete amazement, her head went back and she plummeted to earth on bare land nearly 100 yards over my boundary. In that wonderful moment I knew I had made one of the shots of a lifetime. Holding my bird, I re-joined my friends who congratulated me on this perfect shot. These were proper shooting men acknowledging my moment, in which a routine day's rough shooting had been transformed into a sport fit for princes. Years on, when we meet, one or other of us will hark back to that iconic shot.

left:
Engaging a high bird

On another day, I was shooting during a cold snap over a stock farm in Surrey – of all unlikely counties – and game was scarce. There was, however, a river wending its way through the cattle meadows, which featured several bends under near sheer banks. Wherever the flow was slow, as in the backwater eddies, ice had formed. Where the current hit the river bends broken shards and sheets of ice had built up and scoured the frozen surface of the mud on the banks. The fresh, unfrozen mud beneath was there to be seen and, it seemed, every snipe in the south of the country was there, foraging for survival under the banks.

After the first encounter, I took to approaching the bends from the cover of the adjacent meadows rather than from the riverbank upstream of the bends. A quiet, stealthy approach over the frozen grass was invariably rewarded by the rasping departure of snipe from close under my feet, and the chance of a shot as the small birds jinked and twisted away across the meadows. I shot one or two and missed a lot more.

At length, I put in a stalk on the last bend before the downstream boundary of the farm. I walked so slowly and so quietly that I could hear my own breathing. Approaching the river where the current would be jamming the ice against the bank, and where I just knew more snipe would be holding, I moved in, holding my gun at half

port ready to throw it to my shoulder and shoot. The weight of my anticipation was awesome, and I edged forward trembling with cold and excitement.

I was, of course, nearly on top of the snipe when they got me and went, rising upwards and over the barbed wire stock fence on the opposite side of the river. There was a rare wisp of them. I threw up my gun and fired instinctively at a bird going straight away and it fell. Then, without pausing, I latched on to a snipe that was rising and flying left-handed. Swinging through it, I saw it tumble down. Yes! A right and left: my first right and left of snipe. A few minutes later, having found a stock bridge across the river, I was admiring my two snipe. I stroked the cream coloured breast feathers, and spread their wings. These were no ordinary snipe. This brace were my trophy birds. That was the end of the day's shooting, but the beginnings of a memory that the passing years have done nothing to erase.

A deep, dark winter morning in South West Scotland, and we gathered sleepy-eyed in the farmhouse kitchen. We were going for a morning flight at geese – a first for me. A cup of tea and a Land Rover ride later, our guide dropped us off one by one on the high ground above the loch. My position was at the end of a fir belt, where I was concealed by a dry stone wall. I slipped a couple of fours into my shotgun and waited, shivering in the intense predawn cold. Very soon, the surface of the loch far below became visible and the features of the landscape clearer. Then there was the unforgettable clamour of wild geese making ready for flight.

I don't know quite what I expected, but I certainly anticipated birds that would be far bigger and, well, more ponderous than they were. As it was, the geese in the small skeins were sleek and small, and agile in their flight as they worked uphill towards us, sometimes directly into but more often side streaming the stiff breeze. The first parties went to my right and I heard shots from the guns stationed there, and then others went to my left and were engaged by the guns beyond me. I stood in the cold, rather tucked up and miserable, thinking I was going to miss out on the sport. It was getting light by now and I was expecting the guide to call a halt to the shoot before I had let off a single shot.

Then, overhead, out of nowhere, was a single goose – a great gander. Gun to my shoulder, I engaged him and he came down with a whoosh, thwacking into the branches of the fir trees just behind me. I put down my gun and picked him. I had shot my goose and I treasured him.

An early September day and my friends, who had been at the grouse with me for a week, had gone south. Nothing daunted, I put a piece in my game bag and set out for the hill. That morning I elected to tackle the high ground above Dalcharn and I

was faced with a steep climb from the start over ground too rocky and broken to be ideal for grouse. I kept climbing and worked up a muckle sweat in the process without encountering any grouse, or even seeing sign. At one point we flushed some sheep that had been sheltering from the stiff breeze in a hollow and my black Labrador, Two, made a feint at them before reluctantly slinking back to me in response to my whistle. I watched the daft animals bobbing and bumping away out of sight while taking the opportunity to catch my breath.

I noticed then that I had a few hundred yards more rough ground to traverse, with a deep gully across it, and that on the other side of this there was more heather and less of the broken ground and white grass through which, until now, I had been struggling. In fact, the vista above me was framed by a rising heather-covered shoulder on the left flank with a wide flat out to the right. It looked as if I should take a route up the shoulder and work Two into the breeze so he could hunt up the bonny heather ahead.

The preliminary walk to this included the tendon-bending scramble down and up the gully, and I eventually emerged well winded from this and thinking grimly that in dogging up grouse in the north of Scotland a gun certainly earned his grouse, not that I had even seen one at that stage. After another rest, I started to sidle left-

handed, easing the pain of the climb up the shoulder by angling up rather than by making a direct assault. Throughout all this, I was trying to keep an eye on Two knowing that, on scenting grouse, he would likely pull out ahead of me if unchecked. As it was, he worked close enough and I plodded on, man with dog and gun in that illimitable landscape. I can remember it as if it were yesterday. The sunshine and the wind conspired to riffle the heather and make mirages of the heather pollen. I walked on as if in a dream, my shirt damp with sweat and my shotgun heavy and awkward under my arm. The loudest noise was the rasp of the soles of my boots and the canvas of my gaiters against the heather stalks, and the silence lulled me so that it was as if I walked in an enchanted landscape.

Old Two had no such inhibitions, and quartered more freely on his long legs than he would ever be allowed to do at home in England. In my mellifluous stupor I did not see him catch the scent of grouse; I only realised, too late, that he was picking up speed and roaring on ahead. My whistling was in vain. The sensational aroma of the grouse birds must have been coursing through his olfactory senses, strong, primeval and irresistible. I could only stand in despair as the black dog powered into the crouching covey and put them on the wing. They went ahead, into the wind, and I watched them away in silent fury. Then, I saw Two lope right-handed, dropping down the hill, and feather for a few moments before flushing a single grouse that launched himself into the wind before rolling back and out over the flats downwind. I watched him streaking high over the flats, making to pass me on my right-hand side and far out. I put up my gun and tracked him, and then swung fast through him pulling the second trigger to discharge the choke barrel. That grouse, squarely hit, appeared to fade and fall away until lost from sight in the steep gully.

Recalling the errant Two, I hurried back to the last place I had seen the failing bird, and had the Labrador hunt the dead and hidden ground. I was not hopeful of our chances as there was so much of it, and I had not seen the bird down. However, after some minutes, I saw Two pause and pounce and then return to me with the cock grouse. An old cock, in full feather and with pointed primaries, alone and apart from the covey.

How I savoured that moment! There had been that long walk in and the hard work on the shoulder. Then the black dog had earned a still blacker name by his misbehaviour and I recalled briefly my crushed, miserable disappointment when the covey lifted out of shot. And then the denouement! The big bird had flushed, passing (yes, passing not coming) downwind. I had watched him, tracked him, and then in a moment swung through him as he passed far out, 50 or 60 yards out at least and high over the flats. That was a real hunter's moment, when I achieved that amazing kill. Images of dog, bird, sky and ground all merged and mingled under the warm afternoon sun. It was a princely shot in a land of princes, and in that moment there was but one prince there. I knelt down and hugged old Two for the retrieve and forgave him his earlier indiscretion with the covey.

On our own pheasant shoot, the issue was whether we had held our birds. For sure, we were going to find out that November morning when the three of us, and half a dozen beaters, assembled at Grey Gates Farm to meet our three guests. Six of us was an ideal number as we were to shoot our thin game strips and a few thick hedges, belts, and coppices.

The first two drives really postponed the moment of truth as they comprised two outside locations. The Black Belt may have been a good drive years ago when the farm was larger, but now it comprised a thin ribbon of tall trees with little or no under storey. At best we could expect to flush one or two outlying pheasants and, after placing the guests either side of the belt we 'host guns' made for the flanks. One old cock came forward and was felled, and then a hen bird rocketed up, evaded the forward guns altogether, and escaped. The beaters had tapped down to the guns when another old cock flushed from the ditch and flew back up the belt no more than five feet off the ground. He escaped unsaluted by any of the guns. The second drive involved us surrounding a square block of game cover, which was, to be truthful, badly positioned adjacent to a busy footpath. The manoeuvre went well enough but there was not a single bird in the cover. One pheasant in two drives and it was time for a drink. My co-hosts were, if not panicking, at least anxious to be getting in among the reared game. However, the thin November sunshine was pleasant enough and guest guns and beaters alike

enjoyed their beers from the cool box, and some good craic, one of the hallmarks of a happy pheasant shoot. Only when there were empties did I say to Ken, our keeper: "Deer Leap next, Ken!"

I saw a shadow cross his face. This was the moment of truth.

Ken galvanised his old crew; he was to walk them in from the spot we stood at, while the guns would be driven round by the road. A bit of pushing and pulling, and I got them all into the vehicles. A drive round by the road and into the farm off the road's north corner enabled me to line out the team for the Deer Leap Drive, with the stiff southerly breeze in their faces. We were lined out with two guns to the left of the hedge that bisected the line and four to the right of it. I was positioned on the extreme right of the line and, seeing

everyone was ready, I used the radio to call on Ken to start.

I knew how he would do it. He would bring in the rough grass and the copse round the old pond. Then, he would circle round and bring his crew through the gap in the black thorn hedge leaving old Percy on stop to deter the game from running back into the copse. He would then bring the maize round and eventually out in front of the gun line. I knew Ken would be worrying as he fossicked about in the rough at the back of the drive. There was cover enough there for a seasoned team such as his. However, at least one pheasant took to the wing from the copse – an old cock of several seasons' seniority by the way he flew – flying high and hard back to the big wood behind the left-hand guns. I heard the shot from the other side of the hedge, and then saw the bird plummet earthwards. With that shot we had doubled our bag.

After Ken and his men appeared, there was some delay while they sorted themselves out and prepared to beat the maize itself. I was impatient; I wanted to see if the pheasants were there. This drive was a litmus test for our season. No birds or few birds here would likely mean we had lost our stock. Ken started in and I shaded my eyes with my hand as I watched his team work round, seeing now and then the white splash of their flags or the head and shoulders of the man on the side nearest the guns. They came on and on and nothing happened. My heart sank: it seemed all our work and effort were wasted, and Grey Gates Shoot was an embarrassing flop. I scanned the line. The guest guns were experienced game shots, well able to distinguish a good shoot from a bad one. They would, I thought bitterly, be heading home and telling their other mates that there was not much, no not any, stuff at Grey Gates.

And as my heart reached my boots, the first flush burst from the cover and flew towards the line. They were fine sporting birds, rising and mainly curling a little right to left, and the shots started. I saw a cock bird fall to a single shot and then a hen, the first of a left and right. Here fell a well-taken pheasant, and there a low flier was let through unshot at by the sporting guns. With Ken still well short of the front of the cover, we must have been in double figures and, my blues banished, I felt delighted by the drive. These few minutes were Ken's reward for the hours of hard work and hard slog he had put in, lugging feed and water to the covers and for all that was involved in his good husbandry with the poults since the summer. As I enjoyed all this, I suddenly woke up to the fact that three pheasants had broken out of the right-hand corner of the cover and were heading over the field diagonally towards me. These were for me. Swinging on to the cock in front, I dropped him stone dead and remembered to start the swing again

on the hen now nearly overhead. Leaning back, I took her vertically overhead and heard her crash on to the stubble. A right and left for me! I was still ecstatic when, a few moments later, Ken whistled the ceasefire and I picked up my brace.

Walking over to Ken as if walking on air, I shook his old hand. "Not bad!" I said, "Not bad at all!" He grinned from ear to ear. "Yes," he conceded in measured tones, "there were a few pheasants in there."

High Norfolk in early June, and the pigeons were at the vineing peas. I say at them, and I mean at them. The woodies were homing in on the two 50-acre fields from dawn to dusk. They were a sight to see, thousands and thousands of them flighting in to feed from the woods for miles around. I visited a few days after a mighty pigeon shooter had shot 250 and the June morning was already uncomfortably warm before nine o'clock, although there was a useful breeze that promised to strengthen through the day.

There was a gamekeeper driving round in a pick-up truck when I arrived so, as a matter of courtesy, I made my number with him. He was mildly obnoxious, with a "these fields belong to me" mentality. Whatever his attitude, I was an invitee and there to stay for the day. 'Did I have a dog?' he asked in his surly way. "I have several gun dogs at home," I replied. He looked into my truck as if he disbelieved me and went on his way. I smiled to myself. At my age,

I had buried several good gamekeepers better than he would ever be.

The pigeon shooting practitioners I know all stress the need for lengthy reconnaissance and so, well briefed, I spent some time studying the morning flight lines. It was tempting in the extreme to pitch camp on the south side of the field, but when I waited a while longer I would identify a better line, and then another being even more strongly worked. Eventually, I settled on the Sailor's Belt, as this appeared to be attracting the most persistent flight line. I drove my truck round there and picked a spot to set up my hide. As pigeon shooters are well aware, the setting up of the hide and putting out the whirly gig and flapper all took some time, and it was well after 10 before I was ready to shoot.

This is not an account of what happened during that momentous day's pigeon decoying in Sailor's Belt, but of one bird. I shot all day, and in the late afternoon realised I was about to engage my 150th pigeon. During the day, I had enjoyed every variation of shot in the book, but had taken particular pleasure from the pigeons flighting into the decoys low across the field. As I waited with anticipation for this landmark bird, the flight seemed to dry up and I waited expectantly for several minutes without a chance. Then I saw a single wood pigeon turn in its flight far out over the peas and fly head-on towards me. He came on, as they say, and I made ready to engage him. Finally, he set his wings and made to land short of the decoy pattern. Leaning forward, I took him well out, three or four feet above the crop, as if he was a settling grouse in front of the butts. He went down in a puff of breast feathers, which floated lazily towards me on the wind.

Unloading my gun, I raised my arms to the sky in celebration of my great day and my enormous bag.

North East Scotland in the New Year, and I was one of a privileged team shooting pheasants in the braes of Angus. The birds were too good for me all morning, and by lunch time I was grumpy and wondering why I was there. After lunch, we were to shoot the Bridge Drive, which involved the guns dropping down to the river bank in readiness for pheasants being driven from the woodland and other cover rising steeply on the west bank. My peg was the number one peg – we were numbering right to left – and I was the highest gun by a long chalk with a rising north-westerly gale doing nothing to improve my chances. I could see the gun to my left by the bridge – a Lincolnshire Squire – but I couldn't see any of the other guns downstream of him. It was obvious that if the birds came over me in any number the drive would have miscarried.

Sporadic shots were to be heard downstream and then I saw Squire Lincoln go into action, taking pheasant after pheasant with practised perfection. It was a pleasure to watch him, and I watched with amazement the apparently effortless way in which he dealt with the pheasants curling over him from the far side of the river. I watched and watched as I was well out of it up the hill, and then it happened. A solitary hen pheasant topped the fir trees at the top of the bank and, finding the wind too strong, rolled and turned over my right shoulder. She was at an awesome height – she looked no larger than a partridge – and going a pace when, having turned to my right, I swung through and killed her while rocking back on the heel of my left foot, nearly overbalancing on the steep bank. I recovered to see her go down in an arc and finally fall at the Squire's feet.

That was my supreme shot, my magic moment, the raison d'être of my pheasant shooting. After the end of the drive, I walked down to Squire and apologised for dumping my bird on his head. It was nothing to him; just another pheasant in a long season. I left him picking up all the pheasants he had shot and walked to the game cart carrying my hen pheasant, my trophy bird. Yes! I had killed the bird of the Bridge Drive, as high a pheasant as we had shot at all day. And that one successful shot served to transform my previous disappointment into a day suffused with pleasure as colourful as the Scottish sky under the fast setting, sinking winter sun.

opposite:
Engaging a high bird

above:
The grouse gun

I can look back a long way over my shoulder now and see those shots; the glowing, golden moments of many days spent shooting. In the grand scheme of things it is unimportant whether a quarry shooter hits or misses, but it is much more satisfying to hit. I have not selected these rare incidental successes to show how good a shot I was. It is not an exercise in braggadocio in any way at all. Far from it: as I will go on to admit, the accuracy of my shooting has varied from non-existent (when I was a youth and young man) to rather less than average in my heyday, to even now, with an inherent fragility that on occasion means I miss almost every bird I engage. When disaster strikes, this leaves me, perhaps for one specific drive, dispiritedly picking up a pocketful of spent cartridges with little or nothing to show for them. In a way, that vulnerability

has made the pursuit of quarry species more interesting for me than it is for the brilliant, clinical shot. I never know what the outcome is going to be when I engage a game bird, and that uncertainty makes each shot an adventure. Looking back now, the very act of shooting, the taking of the shots, and not just the days spent shooting, have been a lifelong source of adventure and excitement for me, and that is undoubtedly one of the several reasons why I have enjoyed them so much.

In retrospect, I can picture the locations of all these shots. I remember the black fen, with its reed dykes. I still shoot that farm and, in the many years that my spaniels have hunted that and other nearby dykes, I have never seen another pheasant fly in a way that made it worthy to peck at the same stalk of fat hen as that original hen bird. I have spent hours on the heather hill in Sutherland and taken the same route over the shoulder from which the grouse of my dreams was shot without shooting at another truly memorable grouse. Nearer home, I still walk the woods and fields in which the mighty shots of my shooting career were made. The very landscape of those places is enhanced for me by what went on there in those princely moments, when good birds were on the wing and high in the sky.

I look back now with a sense of privilege that I should have enjoyed such moments and the aura that surrounds each shoot day. It matters not whether those shots were made on a formal driven day, which involved a team of guns, an army of beaters and supporting staff, or during a solitary hunt across the moors of Scotland. All of those days were special for me and the ecstatic, glorious celebratory moments when I had enjoyed the opportunity to make a great shot and had succeeded in taking it simply enhanced what was already wonderful, and inscribed forever for me the pleasure to be had from the pursuit of game.

As I was not fortunate enough to inherit an estate or a shoot, or clever enough to afford to buy one, I can say I have always shot by choice. My enduring, lifelong involvement in quarry shooting has been pursued relentlessly down the years to the exclusion of other rival recreations such as skiing and horse riding, and I have never had cause to regret the path I have followed.

I have observed, with some sadness, those men who have inherited shooting estates without having any reciprocal love of shooting. For some of them, at best, the day's sport is a drudge, a winter chore. They take little or no pleasure from the pursuit, and less interest in its execution. They feel no anticipatory thrill at the prospect of the day's sport. Others see their shoots as a source of income, and get sucked into the thorny path of providing commercial shooting although they have little interest

or enthusiasm for it themselves. On all but the most productive shoots such ventures are likely, at worst to fail completely or, at best, doomed to limp along without charm for the guns or profit for the owners.

For myself, I have not tried to make money out of my shooting: only to keep the cost of it within reason. Save in the first year that I had my fen shoot, I have not had paying guns or run any form of syndicate, preferring to invite guests as a treat for them. In so doing, I have derived enormous pleasure on countless days as host.

And that satisfaction has derived from wanting to be out, be it on high or by days, and from keenness for all the shooting sports. There has simply never been a morning when I would rather lie in bed than be making ready to get out into the fields and woods. I would never watch games when there is the chance of enjoying the pursuit of the shooting sports.

So, as a result of good luck I have been free to move in all sorts of shooting circles and have enjoyed my shooting in the company of all manner and nationality of men, from ferreters, wildfowlers, pigeon shooters and the like, to business moguls and landed gentry. I do not know any one of them who has been consistently keener than I have been. Therefore, I claim that a combination of my good fortune and inclinations has gifted me a princely shooting kingdom. In this respect, I am a man greatly blessed.

Young Guns

I started shooting with a no.3 garden gun when I was eight years old. At the back of the Vicarage in which we lived there was an old timber summer house with a raised wooden floor. Father scattered straw in front of this every autumn, and fed the pheasants with wheat which, in turn, attracted the local rats. They had an ideal setup, with holes under the dry floor of the cabin and a plentiful supply of grain replenished every afternoon.

Father decided I might shoot one of these rats and so, at feed time, I accompanied him as he quietly approached the place. As the straw and the hut came into our line of vision I saw a large rat frozen, as it were, in the entrance to the summer house. I knew enough to keep still but could not resist a glance at my father to see how he was reacting to the moment. "Look at the damn rat boy, don't look at me!" hissed Father, the parson, who I never previously heard swear.

Shocked, I looked back at the rat and, raising the little gun, I luckily shot it dead. Father's unexpected use of bad language was a surprise to me as he was the most mild-mannered and softly spoken of men. It made me realise that there were things he took seriously, and that quarry shooting was one of them. In fact, this was a lesson I had been learning from the first conscious years of my life. I was always aware of my father having shotguns. Also, I recall how some afternoons his friend, Dr Ben Sunderland, would appear and how he and my father would go for an afternoon's rabbit shooting. Too young to accompany them, I remember that they returned with rabbits more often than not – rabbits were plentiful then – and that sometimes there might be some other species of game, such as a hare, partridge, pigeon or pheasant.

The rabbits were prepared for the table by an ancient handyman and gardener called Kemp. He skinned and jointed them in an old-fashioned scullery. I can recall one of my sisters and me climbing into a large laundry basket and watching through the wickerwork sides. Now and then we would lift the lid and the ever-patient Kemp would reward us with an eye or a paw.

My father kept pigs in pig sties – there was still rationing in that immediate post-war period – and periodically one of these would be killed for the table. I was considered too young to watch the pig being killed but my sisters, having planned to watch proceedings covertly from a hayloft, took me anyway, although I was less than five years old. If the experience has damaged me I don't know it, and anyway remember nothing whatsoever about the business. I can say for certain that it didn't put me off pork or sausages! I have mentioned that food rationing was still in force until I was four or five years old, and generally food was still in short supply and of poor quality. My parents responded to this by growing their own

vegetables, keeping pigs and hens, and by foraging in the hedgerows and fields in season as well as by utilising the quarry birds and animals shot by my father.

I mention this to show how early on in my life the link between vegetable gardening, hunting, and gathering, were all closely connected in my mind with eating and food. Growing vegetables, picking blackberries, keeping chickens and shooting quarry were natural, indeed necessary, activities if one wanted a good, varied diet; none of these activities was a fad or an indulgence.

I also remember how, in my first days, my father shot with other men, many of whom came to the Vicarage. Some of these pretended to take some interest in my toy guns, and I was never so proud as when one of them would make some favourable comment. I was, I would say, brought up from the start into the way of shooting, and not just shooting as a remote, occasional activity. The pursuit of game, ground game, and rabbits, was then central to my beloved father's life and I don't suppose there was a day went by without him thinking or talking about shooting in one way or another.

I wasn't much older – six or seven years old – before I was allowed to attend some of the local shoots. One of the first, if not the first, that I joined, took place on a bitterly cold day with the temperature well below freezing. I found myself on the game cart 'helping' the redoubtable old Fred Atherton brace up the birds. Fred had the use of a grey Ferguson tractor and a trailer and he kept the tractor's engine ticking over all day so that we might have a bit of heating. Fred was a great patriarch, having 15 children, and was a well-regarded man about his own village. I can still see him on that day long ago, his face pinched with cold in the freezing wind.

Sometimes I would accompany one of the guns, who was likely a retired military man. There was a retired general – Major General Gerry Skinner – a delightful ebullient man, but a poor shot. Then there was 'Frinkie' – Brigadier Ralph Frink – whose high-flying military career had been prematurely terminated by tuberculosis. A sick man in the post war years, he shot well with a 20-bore and had an understanding of game and game management. He was very kind to me and fostered my interest in fieldsports by giving me a fishing rod, with which I caught countless roach locally. A representative of an earlier generation – still shooting occasionally in my childhood – was one Major K.K. Horne. He had, I believe, inherited a rubber fortune and certainly appeared to be well-to-do. As a young man, I believe he had been a First World War fighter pilot and in the Second, he claimed to have been recalled from retirement to command Duxford Aerodrome. Horne had raced Malcolm Campbell at Brooklands and, in old age, still enjoyed driving a fast car. He had shot dangerous game in different parts of the world and on autumn days would wear a stylish pale green safari suit, which had no doubt been made for him in Nairobi for one of his safaris.

Kaa Horne also had a schoolboy's sense of humour. While at Oxford University he and his brother, Dukey, had attended a circus after dining well but unwisely one evening. There they had taken the opportunity to have a short ride on the circus elephant. Being well oiled, they had refused to dismount at the end of the ride. In the ensuing altercation with the angry elephant handler Dukey had fallen off the elephant and broken his ankle. The next morning the brothers remembered they carried accident insurance and so Dukey completed a claim form. In answer to the standard question as to the cause of the accident he wrote, "Falling off an elephant."

The next question required him to disclose the location, and he responded with "Oxford", and submitted the claim form without further comment. Their next visitors were from the constabulary, who listened to their explanation with some incredulity.

Although I recall Major Horne shooting in the ride way of one Suffolk wood, and killing five jays in a row there in addition to a number of pheasants, he didn't share my excitement at the feat. He was too remote for me to reach and remained a distant,

aloof figure from an earlier age. Apart from these and other retired military men, the local shooting world was well populated with local farmers, many of whom had shoots of their own.

In the village, many of the farm workers – and this was an age when there were still lots of them – would be brushers on shoot days. The local gamekeepers, and there were several of those too, lived in remote woodland cottages on their beats and now and then I would encounter them. At the time of our arrival at the Vicarage, the head keeper on the local estate was one Johns. I remember my father taking me to visit his rearing field, with its ranks of coops and runs. Johns was, it seemed to me as a small boy, a gentle giant of a man, tweed suited even in summer and with, although I may be imagining this, pheasant chicks about his person.

Being brought up in such a strong shooting family, my start with the garden gun soon moved on from rats to rabbits, and I nailed a good one that was lying out in the rough grass of a disused border. For readers who have not encountered one, I will describe Greener's garden gun, as it was a very popular firearm at that time. Mine was a bolt-action single-barrelled firearm that looked more like a .22 rifle than a shotgun. Its distinctive green and white checked paper-cased cartridges had a strange characteristic, which was that the paper case separated from the head of the

cartridge and remained somewhere in the barrel. The sportsman, having discharged the gun, then reloaded and used the next shot to clear the remnants of the paper case from the single barrel. I cringe at the very idea of a similar arrangement being in place on the discharge of, say, a 12-bore shotgun. The garden gun did not pack much of a punch but certainly had its uses against rats, particularly around buildings or poultry, and against rabbits in gardens and allotments. At that time a lot more people, particularly in the country, kept poultry of one sort or another and the rat population thrived, so householders had a continuing and serious need to be shooting as many of them as they could. Although there were rat poisons available, these were nothing like as varied as those on offer today and nor were there any pet-proof delivery systems. There was always a danger of dogs dying after eating the doses intended for the rats.

If poultry keeping created conditions that benefited rats, so did the farm yard barn storage of grain. There was grain to be had in every farm yard as the storage of grain then bears no resemblance to how the job is done now. Although by the mid-1950s the harvesting of corn with a binder and the storage of the sheaves in straw stacks for threshing during the winter months was becoming obsolete, there was at least two old-fashioned farmers with fields adjacent to the Vicarage who had stayed with that system. When the stacks were in the farm yard, as they usually were, the straw sheaves provided wonderful winter habitat not only for rats and mice but also for the local birds.

I haven't thought about the happy days I spent ratting at threshing time for many years, but it gives me more than a twinge of regret to say that it is a sport that has gone forever. For the benefit of younger readers and the pleasure of older ones, I will briefly describe how we went to work. At harvest time the binder cut the cereal crops a few inches above the ground and the harvested stalks and ears of corn were heaped in stooks to dry. While the stooks were in the fields, there was excellent pigeon decoying to be had – more of which I shall recall later. When dry, the stooked corn was collected by means of horse or tractor and cart and stacked in some convenient location. As I have already mentioned, this was often in the farm yard but, particularly in the case of remote fields, the stacks would sometimes be situated in a convenient corner of these close to the road to avoid access difficulties in the winter. These stacks were works of art and were so constructed that the

stooks of corn stayed completely dry until such time as the corn was extracted by the threshing machine. In the meantime, the stacks frequently became the home of rats and mice, although these two species did not, in my experience, co-exist. Where there were rats, there were no or few mice.

I believe that the threshing machine used in my village was supplied by a contractor, who drove his very large machine from farm to farm throughout the locality. However it was organised, I and everyone else in the village knew the day appointed for the threshing of the stack. A day or two before the farmer would often surround the stack, or at least part of it, with scraps of rabbit netting, this being to prevent the rats escaping as the stack was dismantled. On the great morning, there would be a good crowd of onlookers of all ages and many participants looking forward to a bit of ratting. There would also be a few dogs of various descriptions, with a predominance of terrier types. After much greasing and oiling, the massive threshing machine would eventually clatter into action with a great grinding of cogs and whirring of wheels. It was a splendid contraption. When it was operational, the farm workers would start the long job of shifting the stooks with pitchforks and feeding them to the threshing machine so that it could winnow out the grain.

At first, there was little reaction from the rats in the stack, and only the

occasional rodent showed itself. Many of the youngsters became bored and concentrations flagged. On one marvellous day my sister lost interest and, during a quiet period, leant against the side of the stack, quite unwittingly with her shoulder level with a large rat hole. I stood opposite her and still treasure the look of horror on her face at the moment she and I both became aware that a large and inquisitive rat was standing on her shoulder looking for a means of escape. She walked home alone soon afterwards.

As the height of the stack was reduced by the removal of the stooks from the top, the rats descended towards ground level and it was at this point that the sport picked up. As the pitchfork went into a stook it became quite likely that a rat would jump out and bolt for it across the ground adjacent to the stack. In order to make good his escape he had to run the gauntlet of men and boys with sticks and the dogs which, by this time, would be in a ratting frenzy. This was where the wire netting came in, and there was many a wicked rodent that must have thought he had made it only to feel the teeth of the terrier in the back of his neck as he struggled to get through the fence. By the time the stack was down to thigh level, the stooks could be seen to shift as the rats rushed about underneath them. Now, it was possible to kill them with a well-aimed blow from the stick before they had broken cover. In a well-stocked stack, the sport continued fast and furious until the last stooks were thrown into the threshing machine, and then, with the location of the stack marked only by a dry rectangle of straw, it was all over. I remember walking home from such days in the late winter afternoon and enjoying the end-of-day sensation I was to so love on shooting days in the years ahead, with the sense of a good day's sport done.

I make no apology for referring to these obsolete farming practices here because they directly affected my daily life as a young gun. Among the small birds that most enjoyed the then-prevalent farming and household regimes was the house sparrow (*Passer domesticus*). This little fellow always had a bad press in my childhood compared with the tree sparrow (*Passer montanus*). He was a cheeky, vulgarian small bird and, in folklore and fiction, he was also a murderer, if only convicted by his own confession in verse:

"Who killed cock robin?
I, said the sparrow,
With my bow and arrow,
I killed cock robin."

On a less literary level, house sparrows were generally considered to be a much too numerous nuisance that needed controlling. So, when entrusted with my first air rifle, a .177 Diana, Father made it plain to me that I was expected to deploy it against the house sparrows that then swarmed around the Vicarage. The Diana was (and still is) an accurate little rifle, and after some practice at tin cans and the like, I used it to good effect against them. With

hindsight, I don't suppose I even dented the sparrow population, as by then my pursuit of them was limited to such holidays as I had from my boarding school. However, I went after them with added enthusiasm once I knew that they were a nuisance for the mess they made in the eaves of the house and outbuildings, and for their depredations on any feed they could find. My favourite shots involved me concealing myself in the stables and sneaking a shot at the sparrows on the high gutters of the house. An alternative mode of attack was to throw down some wheat for the chickens and take a shot at the greedy sparrows from a concealed hide in the woodshed. On balance, dropping a sparrow from the guttering was the more satisfactory shot of the two.

It was thought by my parents that the house sparrows attempted to dominate the bird table and drive off other small birds. I have never been able to verify this because 50 years on in Suffolk I would describe the house sparrow as a rare bird. I have not seen one here for years. If you think about it, it shows how fragile life is that the house sparrow, so numerous that it became a pest, should have disappeared so dramatically. I probably shot hundreds and another man of my generation that I know, a farmer's son, probably dispatched thousands. Neither of us noticed any diminution in their numbers and yet, in the space of a few years, changes in farming practices and perhaps other changes have resulted in the demise of one of Suffolk's most common birds. Both the farmer's son and I miss seeing our old enemy, while recognising that our children have grown up without missing a state of affairs they have never known – that is, having house sparrows round the place.

Another quarry species against which I deployed the air rifle was the wood pigeons in the shrubberies and belts around the Vicarage. In high summer, young pigeons would perch in the ample cover provided by the leaves of the trees and were the very devil to spot. If I saw one, I would then have to manoeuvre very quietly to find a clear line of fire for a shot. With the .177 having a small pellet, it was necessary to shoot for the head of these wood pigeons; anything less failed to result in a killing shot. Restricting myself to head shots, I missed more pigeons than I hit.

The limitations of the no.3 and the Diana being exposed, I moved on, briefly, to a .410 and then a borrowed 20-bore shotgun. I hit little with the .410 and found it a disappointing, disheartening little gun. I was glad to move on rapidly to a 20-bore and, once that was my gun, I really fell in love with shooting.

I took possession of it in the summer holidays and turned my attention to the sport to be had with the local pigeon population. There were two strategies that could be used to good effect. The first required a dry August and a hot, dusty harvest. With these conditions, the local wood pigeons made for convenient horse ponds and the like in order to drink. I spent many afternoons hidden on the banks of such ponds, enduring the nettle stings and the pestilential mosquitoes, waiting for wood pigeons to flight in from the corn fields. If I was well concealed, I would get good sport and the birds would be easier to shoot than those which had caught a glimpse of me and flared up before landing in the bushes and trees under which I was waiting. It was the sort of shooting in which I, as very much a beginner, bagged up to 10 or a dozen pigeons during an afternoon's sport.

My other approach during harvest was to decoy wood pigeons as they flew in to feed on the stooks, another branch of the pursuit that no one will be able to enjoy today unless combine harvesters are abolished. To the west of the Vicarage there was a grand sweep of fields dropping away gently towards a very minor road. The largest of these fields was really in the middle of nowhere and was greatly favoured by the local wood pigeons. The dry ditch that curved round the top side of it – the side nearest home – had one particularly tall ash tree in it and this was the ultimate 'sitty' tree.

I usually knew just when the corn was going to be cut, an event I keenly awaited, because the cutting and stooking of the corn was the countdown to my sport with the woodies. Once or twice, I was in attendance when the farm labourers entered the field with their scythes. As the binder was off-set to the left of the tractor, the circumference of the field had to be harvested by scythe. The men must have been highly skilled and their scythes razors sharp as they cut this first strip in a very short time and then made way for the tractor and binder.

Only a few years before, harvest rabbits would have provided the local men and boys just as much sport as did the rats in the stacks, but myxomatosis had been introduced in 1953, and rabbits were as rare as hens' teeth in Suffolk at that date for the next decade.

It's interesting to dwell a little on this disease and its impact on the sport of shooting. My father was a keen rough shooter and ferreter, and rabbits were the staple quarry of his sport in the years before England was infested by that foul disease. Picking a page at random from Father's game book, I see that he shot on 16 days between 1 January and 9 February 1944. The bag count was 711 head, which comprised 186 partridges, 134 pheasants, 60 hares, 316 rabbits, four woodcock, five pigeons and one wild duck. The parties on these days varied from one (Father on his own) to eight. The most rabbits accounted for in one day was 81 and the next best 44, with four days of 30 or more. At least one

of the days was spent ferreting as Father recorded that on 10 January he lost his seven-year-old polecat doe.

If those game book entries show rather big bags, there are others that demonstrate how rabbits featured in the everyday bags made by him and his companions. A sequence of autumn walks, mainly over his own rough shoot, records between one and 15 rabbits, most of which were shot over Judy, his beloved border terrier.

I believe it's hard for most of us to imagine shooting of that sort, in which the humble rabbit, while not the only quarry that would be encountered, was certainly the most likely to feature strongly on the game card. According to Father, the standard of rabbit shooting by his companions was extremely high, and this seems likely because he and his associates must have had an abundance of practice.

For today's game shots, who are instructed time and time again not in any circumstances to engage ground game, the very notion that rabbits and hares were shot in large numbers and often formed a large, if not the largest, part of the day's bag must seem very strange indeed. I once asked him if he recalled any accidents resulting from rabbit shooting and he said he did not. It's likely that he and his companions not only became very fine rabbit shots, but also able to assess and judge the safety of their shots in the split seconds they had to do so before engaging any rabbit.

1All in all, it's plain that he and his friends had great fun rabbit shooting and, one suspects, for very little money. His comments highlight the lovely walks on the September stubble fields, the companionship of good friends and minor matters often incidental to his shooting.

Turning six years old in 1953, I am sad to say that my main childhood recollection of rabbits is when, in that year, they first contracted myxomatosis. Walking round the Vicarage grounds with my father my recollection is of him mercifully dispatching numerous rabbits as, blind, immobile, and distressed by that dreadful disease, they waited for the end. For some years it seemed that the eradication had been complete and, certainly, that is why in the next 10 years I grew up in a countryside that was largely devoid of rabbits.

Returning to the sport of pigeon decoying over stooks, it used to take a few days for the wood pigeons to find the stooks and establish flight lines. Once they had done so, I was able to observe the birds winging in from quite distant woods and most of them made their way towards the tall ash tree which, it seemed, they used as a landmark.

I would then enjoy several afternoons decoying. I made a hide in the ditch within range of the tall tree, using leafy ash branches tied together with baler twine, and I designed this to give me a good deal of overhead cover. As instructed by Father,

I always checked to ensure there were no obviously stripped white branches to give the game away. Although I had a few plastic decoys, the real thing was much better, particularly a wood pigeon that had all its fathers and was still of a good, natural and lifelike appearance. Before going out to the shooting area I had cut some thin hazel branches, and I used to pierce the decoy bird under its chin with the thin end of the branch and mount it on the top of the stooked sheaves by pressing the thick end through the straw stalks. With a little practice, I became quite adept at siting and standing the decoys on the stooks in a realistic way, sometimes putting three or four birds on one stook in an effort to create an enticing picture that would draw in a travelling pigeon.

Once the decoys were out, I would run back to my makeshift hide and prepare for action. I really cannot say how many hours I spent in that ditch under the hot summer sun, but I was there a lot. From my hide on the high ground I could see all the way to Wastelands Wood to the south and the Walks to the west. I overlooked a great expanse of ground and could see wood pigeons travelling here and there, and so was often hopeful that one would come my way.

On no occasion did I make big bags, but there were red-letter days when I went home hot and tired with six or eight pigeons in my game bag. I was a poor shot, and so

this bag usually included one or two sitters shot off the stooks or out of the branches of the ash tree. There was something particularly pleasing about decoying over stooks and when the woodies rolled over in their flight and swooped into the decoys I knew well enough that I was enjoying some fine shooting.

Another branch of shooting that my father introduced me to at an early age was roost shooting. In those days the February pigeon shoots were keenly awaited, and there were many participants. I believe that at the start of my shooting career these shoots were not only encouraged but also supported by the Ministry of Agriculture, which supplied free cartridges for the job. Be this as it may, my father used to like to stand with me in the area known as the Thorns in a big wood called Trundley. As its name suggests, this area, which was on one edge of the wood, comprised a compartment of thorns. At that time these were well established, and provided roosting cover greatly favoured by the local pigeons. Another benefit of standing and shooting there was that the thorns were lower than the surrounding woodland, and so the pigeons were more vulnerable than those that swirled around over the taller trees in other areas of the wood.

Here again my bad shooting limited my bags, but at least I learnt the basics of the sport. Father's advice as usual included elements of field craft. He told me I must

opposite:
Young left hander

keep still and, above all, keep my face shaded under the peak of my cap. He instructed me to avoid looking up full face but to peep upwards with my eyes only. His was good advice, which I have applied successfully on numerous occasions over the years while waiting in ambush for all sorts of different quarry birds and animals.

On the evenings my father shot he made good bags, but then he was an exceptional shot and a masterly exponent of the art of shooting. However, one February, he and I both made mistakes that could have been embarrassing. First, my father shot a hen pheasant that he mistook for a pigeon. He declared this to the estate owner, with whom he was shooting. The latter was greatly amused and insisted father take it home and make a meal of it. A few days later this out-of-season hen pheasant appeared as a roast one evening. A week or so later, I capped this by engaging and shooting a woodcock, which I had mistakenly identified as a pigeon. That was an unlucky one as I rarely hit the pigeons, and had never succeeded in shooting a woodcock in several legitimate attempts. I realised it was a woodcock as it dropped from the sky and, to my horror, it did not fall to earth but lodged in a high branch.

In my panic, I fired several shots into it trying to dislodge it, all the time expecting old Jack Ivens, the beat keeper, to appear and catch me with this out-of-season bird. I would have been better to leave it there

because by the time I blew it down, the wretched little carcass was shredded and I guiltily stuffed the remnants of it into the very bottom of my game bag. As it happened, no one appeared and I did not have to own up to my mistake. In fact, I have kept my own counsel on the subject from that night to this. I feel better having made a clean breast of it now.

I have so far concentrated on the sport I enjoyed as a beginner, much of this being the lesser sport through which boys of my era were introduced to shooting. The emphasis was on safety and safe gun handling and, in my father's eyes, that was paramount. He and his associates would tolerate a poor shot that was safe, but never an unsafe shot however accurate it was. There was of course a great deal more rough shooting and rough areas then than there are now, so there was not the need to take a youngster to shoot straight away on a driven shoot. That said, all boys with an interest in shooting wanted to shoot driven pheasants, and some generous landowners obliged by inviting myself and other boys to special boys' shoots. It was usually on these we got our first taste of shooting – in my case mainly just shooting at – driven birds.

The example of my father in all matters relating to shooting was so obviously a good one that I tried to follow it from the start of my shooting career, and still hold to it today. When I have fallen short of it,

I have invariably regretted it. His precepts bear recitation here. First, on receipt of an invitation to a shoot – usually by post in those days – he would reply in the same way by return. Having accepted, he would never back out if he received another, better invitation.

The evening before a shoot, he would make his kit ready to put in his car in the morning. He shot in shoes and always polished these, as he did the smart shoes he wore in the host's house for lunch. He took a spare pair of shooting stockings with him to avoid taking mud into the house. He made sure he had enough money for the gamekeeper's tip, and the correct coins for the sweep if there was likely to be one.

In the morning it was the work of a moment to load the car and to drive quietly and in an unhurried way to the destination of the shoot. When he arrived in the vicinity, he would pull into a favourite lying-up place so that his dog could relieve herself, and here he would always re-check he had everything he needed for the day. This ten minutes lying-up routine ensured he was never late for a shoot and also – and this is nearly as important – rarely early. The last thing his farmer hosts wanted on a shooting morning was a guest gun in the yard half an hour before the time appointed for the meet.

I found this a simple, acceptable routine that has since served me well. Having shot over a wider area than my father

did, I am proud of the fact that I have only exceptionally been late for a shoot when caught in the post-accident traffic jams that affect our trunk roads.

By being with father on formal shoot days, I also received or, should I say absorbed, many lessons in good etiquette and behaviour. He was punctilious about saying "Good morning" and "Goodbye" and, being well organised beforehand, never held up a host keen to draw numbers and get the guns away to the first drive. A naturally talented shot, I rarely saw him poach a bird from a neighbouring gun or even share one. He knew instinctively which were in his arc of fire. He was an adept marker of pricked birds and could direct a picker up to its fall by reference to a bush, tree or some other prominent feature. His judgement as to whether a bird was hit was so good that it was rare for the searcher to return without the bird he had been requested to find. There was no reluctance among local pickers up to go a distance for his pricked birds.

It was with this example that I began my driven shooting career. Our squire was a keen shot and very generous to his shooting friends and their sons. I was invited to shoot with him as a walking gun throughout the Christmas holidays. Some of the days on which I shot were very heavy ones, although my poor shooting prevented me from contributing a great deal to the bag. Occasionally, a drive would miscarry

and the pheasants would fly back to me in large numbers. I remember one drive in a wood called the Grove. A compartment at the back of this rectangular wood had been felled and it seemed that every pheasant flushed turned back over the tall fir trees in the front of wood and curled over me as they dropped in to the coppice. I fired a bag of cartridges without killing a single bird.

On other shoots there was a lot less game, and so my bad shooting was less brutally exposed. I did, however, have a moment of triumph at Ravens Farm, near Dunmow. While shooting at the next peg to that master international shot, the late Albert Steele, I allegedly wiped his eye behind on a hen pheasant. I stress allegedly as it was so unusual for Albert Steele to miss a game bird that I have always suspected she had a delayed reaction to Albert's shot, which made it look as if it was my bird. Either way, the popular view was that it was my bird and for some years in that neck of the woods I was the lad who had wiped Albert's eye.

One farmer shot very late in the day, and

I can still see the flames coming out of the gun barrels of my fellow shots in the failing light of the short winter's afternoon. The consensus of opinion was that he shot too late for the good of his birds, but I think the farmer wanted to get the most value he could out of his brushing team.

A retired Colonel, who had a shoot two villages distant, dispensed with beaters altogether and put us boys, complete with loaded .410s, to cover as if we were a pack of spaniels, while our fathers waited in state on such ride ways as his overgrown wood possessed for what few birds there were in it. In truth, these were very few, as the Colonel preserved foxes as if they were going out of fashion and the foxes ate all his pheasants. Today's shoot captains would be horrified by the very idea of losing lads in cover like this, but the Colonel had had a gallant war, experiencing active service in North Africa and Italy, so no doubt felt that the odd boy was dispensable as a 'battle casualty' anyway.

By the time he was kindly inviting me to shoot, the war had been over for 15 or more years and the Colonel had become rather stuffy. This led to one or two amusing incidents that we irreverent boys much enjoyed. Part of the wood we shot was owned by a laconic pig farmer called Mayfield. On one shoot day, he and I were sent off to walk a hedge and ditch into the wood. As we did so, I spotted a dead fox in the ditch, which had plainly only recently been shot. Mayfield looked at the fox and then rather longer at me, and declared firmly that, "We will not be telling the Colonel about this one."

At that time, the Colonel had as his keeper a retired Army sergeant named Drury, who was the object of frequent abuse from the Colonel, which he appeared to soak up as his due without any resentment. It was rumoured at the time that Drury had been the Colonel's batman throughout the war, and had been the inadvertent instigator of an artillery duel between the Allies and the Germans by shooting a brace of partridges for the Colonel's supper off the roof of a barn in between the two front lines, on the Colonel's orders of course. On one particular occasion, Sergeant Drury had dragooned us ill-disciplined boys into something like a line in the back of a compartment of woodland which it was intended to drive. As the Colonel made his stately way back to us up a side ride, Drury suddenly caught sight of him and shouted in best parade-ground tones: "The line will halt while the Colonel crosses." At this the Colonel was heard to retort, "You silly old fool, Drury!"

This exchange tickled our imagination and, when we shot at the Colonel's, we were always on the lookout for an entertaining incident invariably involving the Colonel or Sergeant Drury or, best of all, both of them together. I last saw Drury at a point-to-point years later – old by then and riddled with cancer. However, I am glad to say he could still swallow the whiskies I bought him in celebration of the fun he had given us in his role as the Colonel's keeper.

The bags made at the Colonels were very modest; sometimes hardly into double figures, but shooting with him gave me some good lessons. His reaction to anyone who was late or scruffy reinforced the importance some hosts place on guest guns being on time and smartly turned out. The cover and lack of beaters demonstrated that a gun with a dog – particularly a spaniel – was at an advantage and would likely get more sport. Finally, it taught us lads that good humour and companionship have an important place in shooting.

Although I shot few birds, these were my first shoots. Now it gives me great pleasure to invite a lad to shoot, and to try to help him make his first tentative steps in quarry shooting. I have helped several boys to shoot their first duck, and watched another youngster wiping his father's eye. I recall a nephew stalking a hen pheasant in the fens, a bird that had concealed itself in the corner of a ploughed field. We all pulled back and watched the stalk, which concluded with a flush as she rose and curled away towards the river bank, but the youngster's swing was true and she entered the game bag with much ado, I can tell you.

Shooting Trials and Tribulations

While thinking on the subject of safety in shooting, I have an ancient incident on my conscience. I was shooting in the fens one extremely foggy day, and was a standing gun awaiting pheasants out of the rough grass and other cover in front of me. I was the left-hand standing gun, with a dyke immediately to my left, on the other side of which was a poplar plantation. After some time, a pheasant rose in front of me too low to shoot and crossed the dyke rising a little above head height, at which point I engaged it. I was horrified when, a few minutes later, one of the beaters' dogs unexpectedly appeared among the poplars. The explanation was that in the fog the drive had miscarried and the beaters had attempted to drive the compartment of poplars to my left. No harm done there, but a salutary reminder of the old adage that you should never shoot where you can't see.

Guns that shoot in East Anglia experience quite a number of birds that would be classed as low on shoots that are carried out over steeper terrain. While guns want to shoot at the best and highest birds they can, the reality is that sometimes guns on East Anglian shoots have to do their duty by their hosts and engage pretty ordinary birds. On one still, flat, poor-flying day I observed a gun who gave the impression that one should not shoot at anything less than 40 yards high.

As a result, he hardly discharged his gun all day and left it up to the rest of us to put the birds in the bag. This we did knowing full well that pheasants were never really going to fly on such a dank day as on that shoot. Those birds were far from being classic driven pheasants, but they still provided some shooting.

As the day went on 'High Bird' looked on disapprovingly, and his reluctance to engage any of the game presented did little to assist our wretched host, who was doing his best to give us a day's sport in less than ideal conditions. The rest of us selected the safe birds and shot the bag. Many guns now shoot all over the country, and those who regularly shoot tall pheasants in Scotland, Wales, Yorkshire and other places no doubt have different expectations to those who mainly shoot in East Anglia.

Having discussed safety issues many times with shooting people, I would say that most guns admit that in each season there is a shot that, while in no way dangerous, is one they 'regret' having discharged. The margins involved between a shot being safe and unsafe are fine at times, particularly when driven grouse shooting. I believe regular grouse shooters have a different approach to beginners. The novice grouse tyro shoots more deliberately, in contrast to old grouse shooting pros who operate more instinctively and at speed against that fast-flying bird. I must confess that on the rare occasions I have shot driven

opposite:
Wanting a wind

above:
Flanking

grouse, I have found the low shooting in front anathema, as it goes against everything I was ever taught. I was not only worried about shooting the beaters but also about peppering the flankers, one or two of whom were, or appeared to me to be, within range long before the whistle had been blown to stop shooting in front.

Shots taken uphill always need particular care. Once, on a pheasant shoot, I was drawn number one, and was a flank gun while a brook was driven. The field rose steeply behind me where its boundary was a public road. Before the start of the drive I noted that feature and that the road was at the extreme edge of my range. During the drive a single hen pheasant made to escape over the field passing diagonally to my right. I killed it with the first barrel. Looking up to the road again, I was shocked to see a cyclist stopped and watching our shoot. I had taken the bird early but, had I left her, with her flattening out and with the hill rising ahead of her, I could have been in trouble.

On another day only one season ago I

was and to get an acknowledgement from me.

In my role as a shooting law solicitor I have occasionally had to deal professionally with the fall-out of shooting accidents. In one avoidable incident the gun concerned – an experienced shot – was walking through woodland adjacent to a disused railway embankment. On the top of this was a public footpath, as he well knew. There was ground cover in the wood and the banks of the embankment were screened by overgrown thorn bushes. A hen bird flushed and made to cross the embankment at head height. The gun took a snap shot and hit a man walking on the footpath, inflicting nasty facial and neck injuries. I have said this was an avoidable accident, and it certainly was. The gun shot where he could not see. He also knew there was a footpath on the top of the embankment and that it was well walked. I remembered that case when, only last season, I was invited to hunt a disused embankment belonging to a friend of mine. I recall that a woodcock, hare, rabbit, and two pheasants all escaped unshot over the top of it, but the compensation was my peace of mind at having avoided adding 'various' to the day's mixed bag in the person of a rambler or child, even though in this case they would have been trespassers.

I acted (as a solicitor) in another case in which the injured child in an accidental

was a walking gun on the left-hand side of a brook, and I observed and noted two standing guns out in the field 60 yards off it. They were on rising ground, well ahead of me and not that easy to see. In fact, it was later in my walk and after I had taken a shot or two that I saw a third gun on the same line, but much nearer to me. He was wearing muted clothing and was, to all intents and purposes, invisible. I was shaken up by this and advised him – he was an inexperienced shot – that he should have given me a wave to tell me where he

shooting was a trespasser. The incident occurred in South Yorkshire in some disused gravel pits. The pits were privately owned and get heavily overgrown with bracken and other cover during the summer time, when this accident took place. The pits were also adjacent to a local housing estate, and the inhabitants regarded these pits as their park and playground.

Prior to the accident, the shooter and a friend had walked one or two bits of cover while trying to shoot a few rabbits. Coming to an area covered in head-high bracken, they flushed a fox and the shooter engaged it in front and shot a child who was walking with her father unseen behind the bracken screen. Fortunately, the pellets hit her legs and she recovered fully, but this shooting was yet another case illustrated by Mark Beaufoy's famous verse, "Stops and beaters oft unseen lurk behind some leafy screen..."

A small number of accidents I have dealt with were caused by guns swinging through the line. Grouse shooting is such a hot branch of the shooting sports that there is always a danger of this happening, and I have noticed that some regular grouse shooters prudently wear pellet-proof goggles or glasses. In one case I dealt with, the gun swung through the line without realising he had done so and was convinced his pellets had ricocheted. Ordinarily a really safe shot, he could not accept that he had 'swung through' and thereby caused that accident. However, all the evidence was that he had done so.

My shooting days have mainly been spent in the company of chosen friends – safe shots to a man – so I have no experience of injuries caused by other guns in the shooting field and little experience of dangerous shooting. But there have been exceptions. When attending a local Christmas holiday shoot as a boy I noticed that the invited guns, seasoned veterans of many days' driven shooting, were reinforced by a new gun. A full-faced man in late middle age, he was dressed in brand new country clothing and had a gun that also looked brand new. He stuck out like a sore thumb. In the field he was downright dangerous, and my poor old father, being drawn next to him, had to suffer him all day, by great good fortune without actually being hit. I felt sorry for the gentleman. A recently retired businessman, he had only just moved to the area. He had been invited to shoot and had accepted without,

I believe, having ever been shooting before.

As a young man I was shooting on a well-known Edwardian pheasant shoot and in one particular drive missed many pheasants, as I so often did then. At the end of the drive, I was looking for a couple of birds I had muddled down, probably trying to delay my return to the gun bus, when the shoot captain came over to me and apologised for the dangerous shooting of the local doctor, who had been standing to my left. "He's a dangerous shot," the captain said gloomily, "but he pays his subs on time so we let him stay on in the syndicate!"

I had been so busy shooting and missing that I had never noticed the man apparently swinging through me time after time. The hairs on the back of my neck rise at the thought of it all these many years later. At the time I think I was rather grateful to him, as his wayward safety standards distracted everyone from my awful shooting.

I also know of two accidents arising from rabbit shooting, both of which demonstrate the danger of ricochet. The first one dates back to the time when combine harvesters had no cabs. What happened was that an idiotic farm foreman shot at a rabbit that was between him and the combine. There was a ricochet. A single pellet deflected from the ground and unfortunately hit the combine driver in his left eye. He lost the sight in it.

In another case, two friends were ferreting and stood 25 yards from the bank in which they had entered the ferrets. There were one or two old iron posts in this bank. A rabbit bolted and one of the two men engaged it when it was exactly opposite him and 20 yards in front. There was a ricochet that hit his friend standing next to him in the face. This accident was so freakish that the victim felt no animosity whatsoever towards the friend who had shot him.

Finally, my father reported an old-time accident that he witnessed during a partridge drive. Two farming brothers were standing next to each other when a hare came forward and passed between them. Brother Tom upped with his gun and shot the hare and his brother. When the other guns remonstrated with him and asked him what on earth he was doing he had replied that he knew he would hit old Harry, but had to get the hare before he did. Perhaps that's what is known as brotherly love.

Father taught me about safety in shooting and imbued in me the etiquette of the sport. However, he did little or nothing to teach me to shoot. A natural shot himself, he had never had a gun fitted and had always killed more than his fair share of the quarry that came his way. He really couldn't grasp my near-total inability to shoot straight.

I was 17 when he took me to Gallyons in Cambridge and bought me a Webley & Scott 12-bore shotgun. Prior to the purchase, I was taken to the Gallyons shooting ground and fired the gun at a pattern plate. The old instructor identified that I had not just a strong but a massively dominant left master eye. He explained that I must either have a cross stock made or shoot from my left shoulder – I was shooting off the right shoulder then. For various reasons I elected to change shoulders, which, at that early age, I adapted to quite readily and I have, indeed, shot off my left shoulder ever since. What old Johnson neglected to tell me was that there was no cast on that Webley & Scott, and that both barrels were virtually fully choked.

When I started to attend driven shoots, my inaccurate shooting was tolerated for several years. Then, in my late teens and early 20s, I would say it began to be noticed. Some hosts were quite understandably exasperated by it, although those that showed it were in the minority. Now and then I would kill a few birds, but not with any consistency. I began to become very disheartened. I enjoyed shooting to be sure. I enjoyed everything about it except my constant missing. Of course, I had no idea why I was missing. The fully-choked

barrels aggravated the agony as, if I did kill a bird in front, I would blow it to bits.

Added to these woes, I was having a tough time in my 20s. Having married young and with two young sons, I was striving to succeed in various ultimately unsuccessful business ventures and was, through my late 20s, preoccupied with the wearisome process of qualifying as a solicitor. Although I continued to shoot, and actually shot for the pot to supplement our rations, I was close to giving it up because I was so bad at it.

I have already mentioned the 'bag of cartridges for no birds' drive in my schooldays and the dreadful performance that I put up that day on the Edwardian shoot. On another day nearer home, I remember a drive in which I missed 15 pheasants in a row. On another evening, shooting September mallard on a fen drain, I was so embarrassed at the end of that effort that I hid in the drain until the other guns had got into their cars and gone home. My shooting was lamentable!

Finally, I made up my mind that upon my qualification as a solicitor the very first thing I would do would be to go to a shooting school for a lesson and that, if I could not improve, I would give up shooting altogether. An instructor named Adrian Perkins was recommended to me, and it was to him I went with my Webley & Scott box lock and my father's old Langley & Lewis side lock shotgun. Perkins

introduced himself and had me mount my gun. He had a look at it and me from the front. Then he asked, "Do you shoot like a prat with that gun, Mr. Barnes?"

"Just like a prat," I replied.

"Well anyone with your eyes would shoot like a prat with that gun; you can't see down the barrels," said Perkins. He went on to explain how I needed to have the guns cast on and the choke removed. He sent me away, and told me to come back in a month's time.

And there, in less than 20 minutes, ended the most important conversation of my shooting life.

By the time I returned, Perkins had had the stocks bent and the choke removed from both guns. One session at his clays then demonstrated I could shoot. I was nearly 30 years old and that was an exhilarating moment. For the first time, I felt as if I could master the art of shooting, the sport I loved so much. I could not wait for the start of the next game shooting season. Since then, I have occasionally and ruefully remembered those frightful drives when the discharge of a bag of cartridges resulted in the one bird blown up in front and an unlucky runner, and what might have been had I been able to shoot half decently then. Had the issues that the perceptive Perkins addressed so readily been dealt with years before on the purchase of my Webley, then I would undoubtedly have avoided many moments of embarrassment at missing. I would also have enjoyed my shooting much more than I actually did in my late teens and 20s.

I am ashamed to say I have never had another shooting lesson. There have been moments when I feel I should have done, particularly after unsuccessfully engaging really high pheasants. Generally, however, since receiving the 'Dr Perkins' treatment, I have usually managed to shoot a few and hold my own in an average team of guns. In short, Adrian Perkins cured the shooting trials of my teens and 20s and enabled me to take full advantage of the next 30 shooting years that followed.

Before leaving the subject of my shooting trials, I would be less than honest if I did not briefly mention the subject of shoot captains and their like. Most of my shooting has been as the lucky guest of generous friends, who, in return, I have then hosted on my own or on other shoots. I have enjoyed the individual characteristics of my friends and the stamp they put on their own shoots as, I suspect, I do on mine. Obviously, if I did not enjoy shooting with my friends then I would refuse their invitations. I have never done that and consider hosting eccentricity part of the essential charm of game shooting.

I have, just occasionally, encountered the so-called captains of syndicate shoots who appear to regard their role to be that of a senior naval officer, and these characters can make a misery of everyone's day. Some years ago I attended a new shoot at the invitation of a friend who was a member of such a syndicate. I was of course introduced to 'the Commander' who, in real life, was an accountant or sales manager or something of that ilk. The Commander ran the day, placed the guns, and also shot in the line.

When we approached the last drive of the day I happened to walk with him towards the cover we were to drive and, being keen to inspect the trout stream that ran along the far side of it, casually requested that I might take the position beside it on the right flank of the line. He consented to this without demur and I enjoyed a few minutes inspecting the river before shooting a couple of pheasants towards the end of the modest drive.

No subsequent invitations to this shoot were forthcoming from my friend, and it was only several years later that he told me my request to stand by the river had been perceived as some sort of insubordination, and that I had been

banned from future participation in the shoot by the Commander. As far as I know, this was a first for me and it goes to show it sometimes helps to see yourself as others see you. Should the Commander ever read this, I feel sure he will take satisfaction in realising this book is written by the bounder he banned.

Over the years, I have occasionally attended shoots owned or operated by very high-powered men – entrepreneurial types. Most of these have been very good shoots, which tick all the boxes so far as game covers, quantity of game, organisation, and hospitality are concerned. Sometimes, the owners have managed the days. Occasionally, I have been embarrassed by the manner in which these high fliers have oppressed their gamekeepers and other staff. When I started shooting, a gamekeeper was always inherently respected and was treated with some deference by his landowner employer. Having seen a number of

stops. At one time I helped run a farm shoot. This was great fun as there were several belts and covers on it that lent themselves to showing a few good birds, if driven intelligently. On shoot days a few locals turned up to beat, and most of them had at least some understanding of what we were trying to achieve. There were, however, always one or two old chaps who just couldn't grasp it at all. When they were beating, they would charge through the cover like tanks, being very vocal. Put on stop, they would be determined to stop the pheasants coming past and would bash the nearest tree nearly hard enough to break their sticks. We all tried to give these fellows an understanding of what was required of them, but it was hopeless; they simply had no game sense at all. They could only march to the drum!

I had thought it could not get any worse than that until, quite recently, 'Ole Tom' featured in my shoot for a couple of seasons. Never a shoot day passed without the old codger wrecking at least one drive. Too old to walk with the beaters, he had to be on stop, and if it was possible to stop in the wrong place at the wrong time and in the wrong way, he would. Finally, after far too long for the good of my blood pressure, he was retired. Our bags increased significantly after he had gone.

I can laugh about them all now, but at the time these chaps were severe shooting trials I wouldn't wish on anyone.

oppressed, put upon keepers being bullied by their nouveau riche bosses, I have always tended to steer clear of them and their shoots.

On every shoot, the skills and game sense of the participants varies, and over the years I have seen it all. The skilled gamekeeper has to deploy his beaters, stops, and so on, not just with regard to the drive he is doing but to take account of their abilities. Nothing is truer in this context than that in connection with the

Lark Farm Shoot

"Ten o'clock as usual, Jim," I said, "and I'll provide a piece." And so it was that when 'the General' and I arrived at the farm shed that Saturday morning, Jim and Colin were already there. Five minutes later, Bill's pick-up pulled up and he and Sam jumped out. Six of us; that was the gun team. There was a certain amount of catching up – we were all shooting friends – and, while that was going on, we took care of some setting up of camp for coffee and, later on, for lunch. The picnic table and chairs were put up and the food and drink boxes and baskets made ready. Spare kit was taken out of the two trucks we would be using for our day on the shoot.

I took a crafty look at the dogs to assess the strength of the dog team. The General and I had our spaniels, Lark and Brandy. Jim, bless him, had two dogs: a pocket rocket of a cocker and a steady old lab. Colin had a lab bitch, not much use I recalled, but better than swimming. Bill had his wild, rangy black Labrador dog, Jake, who could be useful where we were going, and Sam was dogless. Six guns, six dogs! That was a good turnout, and likely to put birds in the bag.

With getting base camp established, and worrying about half a dozen other things, I found I hadn't put my boots on and had to change into them quickly and put a few cartridges in my pockets.

When everyone was ready, the General briefed our four guest guns on the rules of engagement for the day, but mainly on our first cunning plan. We were to go to the east end of the farm to the fields called the Hundreds and try for duck on the Pumping Shed Drain. We had done a reconnaissance on the way in, glassing the drain from the drove and spotting several groups of mallard skulking under the reeds. These would be cut back on both sides of the drain in the course of the winter, which made the duck very skittish, but today the odds were in our favour if we could walk our team on to the drain at the right place.

All the guns except young Sam had shot this drain before, and were familiar with the drill, but that didn't stop the General reiterating the point that the guns were not to shoot on the way across the field. Over the years various briefed guns had been tempted to shoot at hares and pheasants on the yomp over the Hundreds, and I was threatening to get a tie made for this small club of miscreants.

"Do not shoot until we jump the duck off the drain! Keep your dogs back with you! Keep quiet!" The General's orders were clear enough, but I knew from past experience that if a gun can do something wrong, it's likely he will.

Briefing over, we piled into our truck and Bill's pick-up and headed for the Hundreds. It was a longish drive along the drove with the riverbank built up high above us on the right. The fields of our shoot were on the left and below us by quite a few feet. I looked at the black fen soil and was conscious of

left:
In the fens

above:
Spaniels in the fens

how different this was from the heavy land in Suffolk, where I did most of my shooting. There was a deep dyke around every field and most of them were reedy. I noted that the dykes that had grass strips round were wide and rough enough to require two fit, strong dogs to do them justice. I looked out for game and was able to identify one or two cock pheasants deep in the fen, but no great weight of stuff.

On reaching the Hundreds we branched off the main driveway and gingerly took a track into the fen. Then, when we could get no further, we disembarked as quietly as we could. As soon as everyone was sorted, I led the way in single file across the black soil towards the opposite side of the huge field. Three quarters of the way across, we shook out into an extended line 50 or 60 yards apart and, at my signal, started to walk towards the drain, the General at the left-hand end, myself at the right hand, and guests in the middle. The General and I were outside what we had judged to be the location of the wild duck, although we knew from past experience that between the time

against him scenting game, and this proved to be prudent as a young sally hare jumped out of her form just in front of us and made off at high speed for the far field corner. He watched her hopefully, but made no attempt to follow her. No harm done there then!

The line was now fast approaching the dyke and, miraculously, all six guns were in line with dogs at heel. Backs were bent and the final few yards were made in a slow, agonisingly slow, careful half crouch. I hung back a yard and saw Jim, two guns along, looking down into the dyke and then duck jumping out of the reeds. I saw Jim shoot and young Sam next to me and then, just when I thought I was going to miss out, four mallard exploded out of the reeds at my feet and went right-handed away from me along the drain. I mounted my gun and shot the last one – a drake – which splashed into the drain, and clean missed the second duck I tried for which was getting away a bit by then, but still quite shootable.

Then it was all over. The flushed duck had mainly disappeared into the fen as if they had never been there, and I could see and hear my companions casting their dogs out and bidding them to retrieve the fallen duck. Right at the far end, the General's little bitch was working with her characteristic intelligence and energy. I saw her out on the bare land on the other side of the dyke, which was a good effort as many a dog had failed that test, 10 feet down our bank and 10 up the other side, and all through thick,

we glassed the duck and shooting time, they could have moved along the drain or flown off altogether.

I checked the line and it seemed Sam was getting too far ahead. I signalled for him to slow down. Colin's fat bitch was puffing and I could see him giving her a jerk or two with the lead to encourage her to make a better pace. Jim was leaving nothing to chance and had his two on separate leads. I had no idea how he was going to be able to shoot as well. My old springer was plodding along, but I put him on the lead as a precaution overhanging reeds. I saw the bitch pick a duck and head in with it just as I had to slide down our bank while encouraging Brandy to swim back to me with my drake. I then had to give him a heave up the steep bank side and climb up myself after him, thoroughly wet and much stung by nettles.

I then went along the dyke to see how young Sam had got on, and he said he had had a right and left, both birds in the dyke and neither picked. Realising there was serious work to be done here, I called up the General on the radio and requested help. He sent Bill up with Jake, and the big black dog was soon hunting the reeds in

and on the edge of the dyke with his usual boundless energy and enthusiasm. After several minutes he retrieved one of these ducks, and old Brandy the other.

That was Sam and I all accounted for, and so we joined the other guns. All had had a shot or two, and five out of six guns had scored. Only Jim – 'the best shot in East Anglia' – had had the worst moment of his season. With both barrels he had missed a mallard drake the size of a goose, and then had to watch helplessly while Colin wiped his eye in grand fashion. The proud eye wiper was purring with delight at the circumstances of his achievement, and poor old Jim

was looking rueful, as well he might. He had missed a sitter and, being a competitive chap, had been forced to watch his arch shooting friend and rival shoot the old drake he had so woefully missed. Colin's day had started well!

With six mallard in our various game bags – an above-average result for this manoeuvre – we started on the next stage of our day's sport, which required the guns to split into small parties and walk up all the dykes around the Hundreds. If all went well, the parties should work the final dyke towards each other, catching out any pheasants that had run on. I sent Sam diagonally across the field with instructions to head and 'hole up' out of sight in the north corner, and chatted to Jim for a few minutes while Sam made his ground. When Jim and I started I invited him to work his cocker, and the little black dog was soon working a real treat. She was in and out of the reeds and weeds as light-footed as a cat. After some of this, I noticed she went up a gear and began to hunt with real intent. She followed the scent, although all the time keeping close enough to shoot any bird or animal that she might have flushed. Another few yards, and a cock pheasant was flushed and shot out over the water. The little bitch looked to Jim for instruction and he allowed her to make the retrieve. She jumped into the dyke and had to secure the cock bird, which was still flapping on the surface film. She swam back with it and brought the bird to hand to

complete a red letter sample of spaniel work. Jim was thrilled to bits and his miss at the drake forgotten in the exhilaration, at least until Colin reappeared. I was really pleased for him, as I knew just how hard he had been working with wee Jess throughout the close season.

After Jim's cock bird had been stowed in his game bag, I suggested he rest Jess and walk 10 yards out in the field and 30 yards ahead with Jess at heel. I explained that I would work Brandy in the lesser dyke that formed the northern boundary of the Hundreds. This was a narrower, smaller dyke with less cover, and I was quite surprised to spring a pair of teal. I shot one of these and Jim the other as it bounced skywards in a characteristic teal-like way. We continued down the dyke and I approved of the way in which Jim, the most astute and experienced of my rough shooting friends, held his position throughout our walk along this dyke and kept an eye on Brandy for advance notice of any bird that the old dog might put up out of the reeds. Most guns would concentrate for the first 100 yards, and then let their attention wander so that they were surprised by a pheasant or duck being flushed.

We were now approaching young Sam's hiding place and I was expecting him to have some action. Sure enough, a cock bird rose well ahead of us and took a diagonal line past him. The bird presented a long, low shot, of the sort one would forbear from

shooting at on a formal driven day, but a typical, difficult chance in the wide-open spaces of the fens. My money was on the pheasant, and I was right to put it there. Saluted by two barrels, the old cock flew on unscathed. On reaching Sam, we took the last dyke down towards the other party and, again, I was again careful to have the guns walking where they were most likely to be able to get a shot. As the two teams approached each other we holed up a couple of hen birds. I let one of these go as it did not present a worthwhile shot, but another one attempted to curl back and was shot well by Bill as it went right-handed of him.

We finished working this last dyke close to the vehicles and went back to base to hang up the game and have a beer. We had six mallard, two teal and one hen pheasant to show for our efforts, and the reservoir to shoot before lunch, so we did not linger back at the barn. The breeze had stiffened a bit by now and that was all to the good, I thought, as I placed the guns at strategic points behind its raised banks. I had stressed to the guns that while they must not show themselves, they would find it beneficial to go at least a third of the way up the bank in front of them. Once the guns were placed, I had a word with the General on the radio and gave him the go-ahead. He must have showed himself, as a few moments later there were wild duck over the water and climbing as they left the pond. A brief fusillade of shots later I saw three duck tumble out of the sky as the rest departed the scene. Then there was a pause in proceedings until another group, and then another, rose and went out into the wind. Some swung round and came back higher, and two of these dropped with a splash into the water. Another shot or two all round, and we called a ceasefire.

The dogs then came into their own yet again. I had Bill put Jake to work on the mallard in the reservoir. He was the dog for that job. Then Brandy and the General's little bitch were deployed in the reed beds around its sides. The other dogs were used for searching the adjacent fields and drains.

Our pick-up took the best part of half an hour, and with 13 mallard and a single gadwall we were satisfied we had accounted for all but two of the ducks we had shot, and would try for them later in the day as I intended to hunt the drain into which they had dropped.

Those of us with game bags were glad to take the weight of the ducks off our shoulders by the time we got back to the barn. We hung them up in the shade with the ones we had shot up on the Hundreds and had a drink and a sandwich.

While 23 head of game would not satisfy or suit many driven game specialists for a morning's shooting, the consensus among us was that we had had a great morning's sport. We had walked away and worked hard for our shots. Apart from one or two lapses, the dogs had worked well for us, particularly the diminutive Jess.

Basking in the late autumn sunshine, I felt like the luckiest man in the world. I was hosting a day without hassle or pressure, and my guests were not just guests, but were among my closest friends. As we sat in the sunshine and chatted, mainly about shoots and shooting, I felt the day – my sort of day – stood comparison with and compared favourably to some of the industrial shoots that are carried on for profit. After all, I was thinking there is nothing better than to share a day's shooting with one's friends. There was a moment then when, with us all feeling so relaxed, we might have packed up, but the prospect of the afternoon's sport was to overcome such indolent thoughts. For the first time in several seasons, I had sugar beet in the ground in the last week of October. The Nursery field, Hungry Hill and Black Dyke all had beet on them and so there was a great chance to see what the dogs could do.

Having been feeding Black Dyke, I wanted to start there first and, as it was essential to have heading guns to stop the pheasants running on, I allocated that role to young Sam (no dog) and Colin (useless dog) and took the rest of my team along the back boundary of that field. I then needed one dog on the left-hand dyke, which left me three other guns to take a thin strip of sugar beet adjacent to it. To put it mildly, I was undermanned.

Although it was now early afternoon on a pleasantly warm October day, there must have been some scent because the dogs started to wind themselves up as soon as they were ordered to hunt in the sugar beet. With the amount of whistling and shouting going on, I thought it would not be long before there was a run in and Bill's dog, Jake, was the first to go. He just put his head down to the ground and took off along a wheeling in the beet at full speed. He flushed the cock pheasant he was following 80 yards from the standing guns and young Sam took a fine, high shot, a classic driven bird on this the roughest of rough shooting days. By this time Jake was enjoying a glorious riot and

attack the outside strip of Nursery field. This involved a long walk for both the heading and walking guns, but on the way, my walking team floored a couple of mallard that had been resting on a quiet drain. I had not seen mallard there for several years, so thought that was a bonus. The beet at the far end of Nursery proved to have a very heavy, high top to it with the leaves coming up to thigh level. While struggling through this I noticed Brandy beginning to slow down, and could see that the other spaniels were also running out of steam. They seemed to have a revival when they scented a cock pheasant in front of the heading guns, which they eventually flushed. One more pheasant in the bag!

That left the two mallard to pick from the distant dyke, and I assigned Bill with Jake to that task as the latter still had plenty of go in him. Jake retrieved one duck, but there was no sign of the other.

And with that we shouldered arms and walked back to the barn. With the dogs all done that was the end of our day at Lark Farm. I had enjoyed being on my shoot. I had taken pleasure in having my best friends to shoot with me. I had relished working my old dog. I had happy recollections of my hits and misses. In all it had been a good day, a typical Lark Farm foray.

We cleared up at the barn and then laid out and counted the bag: 28 head and a predominance of mallard making up the bag, which we shared out between us. By

was hunting free on the far side of the field, which was a shame as that was where I had planned to go next. The spaniels seemed to be infected by Jake's jaunt and were all hunting energetically but with scant regard to their owners, all that is, except Jess, who was still looking to Jim for instructions.

A combination of the rioting dogs, thick cover and general confusion meant that although several birds were flushed only one more pheasant – a hen bird – was accounted for and several others escaped unshot at or were missed by the guns. As only Jim's Jess had behaved during the drive he was glowing with pride about her, rather to the disgruntlement of the rest of us.

As Jake had hunted out the next drive during his unauthorised riot, I decide to walk to the far side of the sugar beet and the time we were on the road home the spaniels were asleep in the back of the truck. They had had their day.

Another time, on another October morning, on my way to the office I felt the wind blowing. As I worked at my legal files, and listened to the interminable tales of my clients' matrimonial troubles and disharmonies, I kept looking longingly out of my office room window at the scudding clouds and the lowering sky. As I looked at the sky, my mind's eye was down at Lark Farm. All I could think was that the duck would flight that night, and the stronger the wind the better. As I sat in that dismal office I could see the wild duck flying across Lark Farm on their evening flight path to the lagoons on the edge of Ely. It was easy to visualise how they would, on such a rough night, turn as they crossed the river and flight in to my waiting gun. Usually, they would pass over the river high in the sky, scarcely turning their heads, but I knew on such an evening the temptation to drop into the river would be too strong to resist.

At length, so it was for me too. I had appointments in the diary. I called my secretary in. "Cancel them!" I said. And then, slinking out of the office, I went home and changed into my shooting clothes, put my gun and cartridges in my car, and drove down to the fens. On the main road, the wind was so strong it was buffeting the car and I grinned to myself as I looked forward to a stolen hour to myself and the evening flight.

As I came to Lark Farm the sky was darker still, and lowering, and the clouds raced like demons in the late afternoon sky. Soon, I was on the river bank adjacent to Lawrence's Farm, where there were the remnants of an old cattle yard and buildings. It was a lonely spot and Lawrence and his kin, who had worked this fertile land, had long since left it. Only the outline of their toils now remained in the black fen.

I made careful preparations against the coming of the duck. I picked a spot where I could stand with my back to a willow bush. I trimmed some branches from this so that it gave me cover from duck flighting upstream heading into the freshening gale. To my immediate right-hand side the main bund that formed the river bank rose up so high that I could not see over it. I was stationed on the river's edge and, where it flowed past me, palings protected its banks. I would have to be careful, as my dog would have difficulty in clambering over these with a duck if sent for a retrieve in or over the river.

The river itself was a little over 30 yards wide, and the far bank was reed and nettle covered in what was a minor wash that would take surplus water in times of heavy rain. This afternoon the current was confronted by the gale and there was a good slap on the surface of the water. That was just what I wanted.

As the light dripped out of the autumn evening, I waited for the flight to start and watched the denizens of the river and its banks go about their business. Moorhens croaked from time to time in the green rushes on the far bank, and now and then I would see their black shapes or white tails in the margins. Flocks of tits, warblers, and other small birds flitted nervously among the scrub branches and in the reeds. A barn owl flew over the bank, scattering them and passing a few feet above my head. Cock pheasants showed fleetingly on the top of the bank, their silhouettes still only for a few moments as they prepared to fly the river to jug in the warmth of the wash.

When, in the higher sky, I saw the evening flight of crows, I knew it would not be long before the duck came. I gripped my gun more firmly and scanned the sky and Claire, my black Labrador bitch, quivered with anticipation at my feet. The light had nearly drained away when the first pair

came and I spotted them when they were way down stream and high over the river. I actually saw them look down and veer left-handed to find a flight path up the river towards me. They flew over the very middle of the river and were dropping as they approached my position. Leaning forward, I fired at the second duck and killed it cleanly, only to miss the one in front as it climbed and swerved past me in a second. Claire looked to the bird opposite us in the water and I sent her for it. She went with a bold leap and returned with it after a short swim. As she could not get out, I put my gun down and hauled her over the palings. Other duck were now showing and some were landing way downstream of me, while others were in my vicinity. As it became darker, I concentrated on those duck that were flying no further out than mid-stream or, better still, over my head or even out to my right.

I was shooting straight and counted my bag as I compiled it. A duck down in the river and Claire went in again, returning puffing and blowing, and again I put my gun down and, taking the mallard from her, hauled her on to dry land. Then, there was one that flapped into the far bank and I heard her swimming in the reeds there before she reappeared, this time with another fine drake. I had several shots over my right shoulder and heard rather than saw the duck from these come down either on the drove or into the field below it. I had four from the river at my feet and five to pick from the drove, or thereabouts, and then another one, the last one, a blur of a duck straight overhead and down on the top of the grass bank with an audible thump.

And then it was all over. There were no more duck moving; the flight was done. I unloaded and bagged up the duck Claire had already collected, putting these in and taking out my flash light. Then I had her pick the last duck, which had fallen just behind our position, before we searched for the five that were somewhere underneath the bank. For a while these seemed to have vanished, but then the bitch started finding them in the rough cover on the edge of the field, and it turned out there were three there and two that had fallen further back on the edge of the drove. When she emerged out of the darkness with the 10th duck I gave a silent cheer. I was all picked up.

As I drove home, I savoured this red letter flight as I had never before achieved double figures. More often, I picked up three or four at most, and so this night was quite exceptional. I replayed it all in my mind, from the rumbustious wind to the mallard flying towards me, dropping and banking, making into the gale and the satisfaction of good shots achieved. I glowed at the game and effective efforts of my black bitch and spoke her name with affection. She thumped her tail in warm response and, at that moment, as so often before and since, I thought shooting the best pursuit possible in this small island of ours.

The Feed Ride

Before the start of each season, Father would have the local chemist make up in a small bottle a mixture of essential oils. Aniseed featured strongly in it, but there were other, secret ingredients. A drop of this medicine was added and well mixed into the daily bucket of wheat that he fed to the pheasants, and I can still recall the strong, distinctive smell of it on the corn.

The Vicarage grounds comprised nearly seven acres of paddocks and shrubberies, all enclosed within a mature belt around the circumference. Apart from the hard woods, many by then being nearly 100 years old, there was game holding cover in the form of such shrubs as yew, box and snowberry. On his taking occupation, some of the paddocks had been planted and these areas, at that time, provided perfect, warm habitat for pheasants.

The head keeper of the local estate was happy enough to have an enthusiastic amateur keeper in such a strategic spot, and in the autumn, straw bales would be delivered and taken out to the different feed rides. Father liked a long ride, which he said stopped pheasants squabbling. He would for preference make his straw ride long and narrow. By each ride, he kept an old fork and sometimes a rake.

In the late autumn, the pheasants from the surrounding land used to draw into the Vicarage grounds, attracted by the warmth, shelter and quiet, and also by my father's feed rides. He was home based and so liked to feed mid-afternoon. His practice was to draw a big bucket of wheat from the bin and mix his medicine in this very thoroughly. Then he would walk round his three feeds. On reaching each one, he would first shake up the straw, then feed the corn, and finally shake up the straw again. The object, he explained, was not just to feed pheasants but to hold them and, as far as he was concerned, the longer they had to spend scratching in the straw to locate the grain, the happier he was.

As a small boy, I loved to accompany him to the summer house feed, which could be approached discreetly by a path through some laurel bushes. A stealthy walk in would let us look on to the feed ride and see if it was occupied by pheasants which, at that time of day, would likely be feeding hard and trying to fill their crops before a long night at roost.

As the winter days became colder and the winds keener, more and more birds migrated to the Vicarage grounds for the shelter and feed they could find there. At length, in December, there would be a drive from the Vicarage. The whole grounds would be worked round and the pheasants driven out of the south-west corner over lower ground, where they provided splendid shooting. As the best bag from this drive was in excess of 70 head, and the pheasants flew well, the Vicarage Drive had something of a reputation locally.

opposite:
Hatching

One recognisable hen pheasant proved to be very sharp when the Vicarage Drive was being shot. She would slip into the hen run and stay there until the beaters and guns had gone. She well illustrated the way in which pheasants learn from their experiences in the course of one or more shooting seasons.

In my father's time, several pheasants nested in the garden and grounds. One particular hen pheasant nested for several seasons under the cover of a bush that grew against a wall in the vegetable garden. I fed this pheasant regularly and she became so tame that she would take corn from my hand.

Although the local estate was well keepered, and vermin control, including the running of trap lines, was routine, the nesting birds were vulnerable to predators of one sort or another, and Father's finding and monitoring of the nests in the grounds demonstrated this. I remember one nest that was positioned up against the rabbit netting fence of some new plantings. We had located and kept an eye on this nest for several days. It had more than a dozen eggs in it. Then, one morning, we found the nest site much disturbed and several eggs broken. The head keeper was called and, after careful examination of the evidence, he placed strychnine in one of the remaining eggs. The next morning the culprit lay dead on the nest it had been

claws into the bantam and decapitated her, before turning her attention to the chicks, which were by now without their mother protector.

While today's gamekeepers regard the fox as their worst enemy, in the days of my childhood the stoat was undoubtedly at the top of the list of predators dangerous to game. The tunnel trap was in routine use, and until the prohibition that meant a gin trap, which was a highly effective tool for that job. Gamekeepers then walked much more than they do now, and a gamekeeper habitually carried a shotgun, which enabled him to squeak and call in almost any stoat he encountered in the course of his rounds.

At Lark Hall Farm, I once chanced on a weasel harassing a brood of newly-hatched partridges. It had these in the open in a field of recently sown onions and it was only my lucky arrival that prevented a bloodbath. Having quite frequently seen stoats carrying rabbits of different sizes with apparent ease, it strikes me it would be interesting to work out their power-to-weight ratio. They are enormously strong.

There is a story still in circulation about the fate of a gamekeeper on the famous Six Mile Bottom partridge shoot many years ago. I do not know whether it is apocryphal, but it goes like this. A beat keeper was due to meet the estate's land agent one afternoon to show him his partridge nests. The keeper walked his beat and checked all the nests in the morning. Returning in the

destroying. It was a hedgehog. When I read these days of the well-meaning but misguided activities of hedgehog welfare societies and the like, I remember the old keeper's remedy for nest robbing. I cannot help wondering how many of the nests of stone curlew and other iconic birds are destroyed by protected hedgehogs today.

Another predatory strike occurred at the Vicarage while my bantam was acting as stepmother to a brood of baby partridges. In this case, the culprit was a barn owl, which had a family of her own in a nearby windmill. This owl tried to attack the young partridges in their run, and the brave bantam stood her ground while the chicks hid underneath her wings. The owl got her afternoon with the land agent, they found a recently deceased hen partridge and her nest that had been attacked by a stoat. The keeper was sacked on the spot. This story is retold from time to time. Sometimes it is a keeper who tells it to show what a hard life gamekeepers endured in those days. In other circumstances, it is landowners who want to demonstrate how difficult it is to sack an idle or incompetent gamekeeper these days. Whatever gloss is put on it, there is no getting away from the fact that stoats were given a hard time on partridge manors, and wild partridges thrived.

I remember reading a shooting book of that era in which the author argued how bad it would be for the image of shooting if shoots had to resort to rearing and releasing partridges. In fact, he regarded the possibility as quite absurd. Then, the partridge was in a similar position to the grouse today: wild stocks of the species vary from year to year depending on the success of the breeding season, as we are well aware, but which with effective, conscientious management, generally thrive. I have no doubt that the author of that book would be amazed and horrified if he were to revisit the wild bird shoots he shot over in his day. He would have to walk a long way now to find shoots devoted exclusively to wild birds. All the shoots that relied on wild partridges and pheasants for their sport would now have pens of one sort or another for the release of game prior

to each season. The widespread practice of releasing poults has of course shifted the emphasis of mammalian predator control from mustelids to foxes. The fox is now without doubt regarded by the gamekeeper as his main enemy, and with good reason. Anyone who has seen, as I have more than once, the depredations of one fox or, worse still, a pair of foxes around a release pen, will appreciate the damage they are capable of doing. Many articles, books and videos have been published and produced by the many skilled practitioners of fox control and it's not my intention, as an amateur, to offer any advice or instruction on this subject at all. However, as a shooting man and deer stalker, I have encountered many foxes and have had to protect my game birds and those of my connections.

During my last two seasons at Grey Gates Farm, I and my associates had serious issues with foxes around our release pen. In the first season, I located the den – an old badger sett – in which the fox cubs were housed. I erected a temporary high seat and sat up on successive evenings. On the first of these the vixen did not come, although the cubs emerged and played about on the short grass at the entrance to the den. On the second evening, the cubs came out a little while before it got dark and the vixen came in at speed to feed them. I was able to call her away from the cubs and accounted for her in a wheeling 50 yards in front of my high seat. I returned the next evening

hoping to get the dog fox but never saw him, and have the impression he must have moved the cubs elsewhere as the den then fell into disuse.

These events led me to suppose we would have trouble from this lost litter when the poults came, and we did. Our fox man came with the lamp and rifle and accounted for several, but it was plain from the poult carcasses we were finding that we had not shot the last one. One morning, I visited the pen before first light and climbed on to a row of big bales. As the light came, the pheasants in the release pen wood began to make a commotion. My guess as to what was going on involved two or three foxes working the poults, but I don't know whether this was the case as when a fox came out in front of me with a poult in its mouth, I shot it.

Before the start of the second season, I never found a den at all and there was little or no evidence of foxes about the farm. However, recognising that there are many hours of the day when none of us were there, I decided to deploy that main

above:
Rearing

traditional weapon in the gamekeeper's armoury, the fox snare. I elected to run a snare line on a speculative basis in the vicinity of our pheasant pen.

I was quite methodical about this, first buying and then weathering a bunch of free-running snares. Then I had a local engineer make me some metal stakes, which had a hole for the snare wire in the top of each one. I weathered these stakes too. As soon as our poults had been delivered, I set the snares in runs near by the release pen. These were not all fox runs; after all, the evidence was we had no foxes, but these were the runs that I thought it likely visiting foxes would use. The outcome of this was the catching of no fewer than four foxes within the first fortnight and, happily, the substantial elimination of fox predation for the rest of the season. A high percentage rate of return was achieved and a great shooting season had by all the guns. As I buried the snared foxes I was reminded most forcefully that a snare works 24 hours a day, every day. No gamekeeper, however conscientious, can compete with that.

The satisfaction that the gamekeeper – be he professional or amateur – derives from snaring a fox has, at its root, the feeling that he is controlling his ground and protecting his birds even while he is absent. His silent fox catching device is at work whatever else he is doing, or wherever else he may be. The use of terriers against foxes is of course the complete opposite of this and, over the years, I have occasionally enjoyed this method of fox control as a country sport in its own right.

The dykes at Lark Hall Farm have been dug out of the peat and the sides of them are readily and not infrequently excavated by foxes wanting a den. Certain dykes are more favoured than others, and one favourite bisects a strand of sandy soil in which the crafty foxes find digging extremely easy. I try to visit Lark Farm every February or March to walk the dykes in the company of a terrier man. I have had some great sport with the bold, brave little dogs and done my breeding stock of fen pheasants, such as it is, a few favours as well.

I well remember my first such visit, years ago, with two characters called Scurry and Hutch and their foxing terriers, the exact breed of which was difficult to identify with any degree of certainty. Anyway, they seemed game little dogs and I took them and their owners to each earth I knew of in turn. At each one, the dogs investigated the mouth of the holes and then cocked their legs and peed on it. Having brought Scurry and Hutch some distance, I was understandably disappointed by these blank draws, and so took them to the last chance earth, where the den was in the dyke with the sandy sides.

On reaching this, Scurry's terrier marked straight away and started scraping at the hole before squeezing inside it. His barking became fainter as he went in further, and eventually he stopped and could just be heard barking and growling 15 feet out under the field. Here Hutch came into his own with the spade, digging out a hole above the dog in just a few minutes. Stopping now and then to check that the dog was still in the same place with his electronic ferret finder, he soon opened up the top of the tunnel which disclosed the back of the terrier moving backwards and forwards as he vigorously worked the fox. As soon as the terrier withdrew, Hutch told me to stand back and be ready. A few seconds later a dog fox leapt out of the hole and made to run across the drilled wheat. I had him before he had gone five yards. After that excitement, Hutch replaced the soil he had dug out, finishing off his work by replacing the divot with the growing wheat in it. That was my first experience of terrier work.

With Lark Farm being remote from my home, it was not always possible to find a terrier man who could spare the time to come with me. I would then try to borrow a terrier, and it was while in possession of a loaned terrier that I became involved in what I have always referred to since as the Gorby Gumming affair. Scurry was at the heart of that caper, as he so often was, because while he said he was too busy keepering at home to visit Lark Farm with me, he did have a dog in his kennels he would lend me. It was not his best terrier,

opposite:
On the feed ride

above:
Adversaries!

he said, but it was a strong dog called Gorby. This was not an attractive animal but, on the basis that beggars can't be choosers, I picked the dog up the following Saturday morning and drove him down to Lark Farm. I was on my own that morning and so was heavily encumbered with gun, spade, probe and other equipment. I took Gorby round the usual fox holes, but there was nothing that interested him and he marked hole after hole with copious squirts of pee. Then, he marked a hole I had only visited as a last resort and tried his best to get at the fox inside but was, to his fury, prevented from doing this by the small size of the hole. I would have to dig. Gorby could get his own length inside the tunnel but no more, so I dug the first hole, a yard in to the field from the top of the dyke bank. By the time I broke in, Gorby was on my shoulder and dived into the tunnel through its freshly broken roof. He drove the fox back another yard and could get no further, so I had to dig another hole a further yard into the field with Gorby supervising again, and jumping in to engage the fox as soon as I broke the crusted top of the tunnel. This process was repeated no less than five times as the fox retreated until he could go no further, and Gorby was able to engage him at close quarters. Then there was mayhem in the tunnel in the bottom of the last hole with fox and dog scrapping and snarling, until I was able to assist Gorby. A moment later, and Gorby was pulling the fox out. When at last he let go of it, I looked at Gorby's face and snout, which were covered in blood (although I couldn't tell whether the blood came from the dog or the fox) and soil.

I remembered reading that the handler should always inspect a foxing terrier's gums after it has been working and looked at the inside of Gorby's mouth. His gums were uninjured but I looked once and then twice at both sides of his mouth. He didn't have a tooth in his head!

An hour later, back in Scurry's yard with the terrier, I found Scurry mending a puncture. He straightened up and, when he asked me how I had got on, had a sly look in his eye. By way of reply, I held up the remains of the big dog fox. Scurry shook his head in disbelief, looking from me to the fox to Gorby and back all over again. "By goom!" he said at last, "Gummed him to death, did you Gorby?"

Throughout my shooting life I have shot a number of foxes with my shotgun. I have no objection to this on, say, a fox drive if loaded with suitable specialist cartridges having heavy shot, at least fours and better still, BBs. However, I have to say I don't like shooting foxes on formal shoot days when I have to deploy an ounce or an ounce and a sixteenth of number six or seven shot. A game load is for shooting game, and is far from ideal for deployment against an animal as large as a fox.

One gamekeeper friend had to carry out fox control on and in the vicinity of a stud farm, where many valuable thoroughbred mares grazed in the paddocks. He became so concerned for their safety that he abandoned his centrefire foxing rifle and took to using a wildfowling shotgun chambered for three and a half inch cartridges as his lamping firearm. He claimed this was effective against foxes out to 70 yards. He was a man skilled in field craft and would, I am sure, have been able to squeak his foxes in that close so his was a good solution in that locality.

Although I used to lamp and shoot a number of foxes, that practice does not tie in well with my deer stalking activities, which require me to be up early and out on the ground before it is light in the morning. However, I would say it is while deer stalking in the woods and fields that I have had my most interesting encounters with foxes.

In the spring and early summer it is not uncommon to see a fox carrying his or her kill. Invariably, such a fox moves

above:
On the wander

deliberately and with a sense of purpose. This is the vixen or dog fox taking food to the cubs. I have watched such a fox several times and, if there are known dens in the locality, it may be better from a game protection perspective to watch rather than shoot the fox on the first occasion it is viewed. He or she may reveal the whereabouts of the den. I have found, however, that a fox carrying a carcass will stop to a squeak. On one occasion I saw and shot a fox carrying the carcass of a half-grown muntjac doe.

In the summer time, when waiting for deer, I have kept an eye open for foxes that might emerge from runs or show on short, cropped grass in the vicinity of rabbit warrens. One of the farms on which I control the deer has a number of well-established mown grass paths and the local foxes prefer to use these in the early morning to avoid getting wet in the long grass. When walking on these, their whole bodies are visible and they are very vulnerable to a shot with the deer rifle off the bipod.

By harvest time the year's fox cubs are getting about, and these sub-adult foxes are naïve and often present the chance of a shot. I remember examining one lightweight specimen at Grey Gates Farm one morning after I had sacrificed my chance of a shot at a deer to deal with him. For a moment, I wondered whether it had been worthwhile to trade the two chances but a glance at the cub's teeth and his proximity to the pheasant release pen was a sharp reminder that today's silly cub is tomorrow's voracious pheasant-slaughtering fox.

From then on, with the corn cut and the cover reducing by the day, I have had great sport from my high seats with passing foxes. Invariably wearing a squeaker on a lanyard, I have used it to good effect and brought in distant foxes and dispatched them. The centrefire rifle certainly messes them up and I have no hesitation in saying I get more buzz from shooting a fox that I do from engaging any deer.

Moving from mammalian to avian predators, I will start with the common crow. The habitual presence of these birds on a regular shoot is an affront to good game managers. Handling these birds gives a person the chance to study their massive powerful beak and, if they are alive at the time, their propensity for using it. I have deployed the Larsen trap against these brutish birds to good effect. In the spring, I made it a practice of regular visits to the shoot to identify the territory of the paired crows, and I have always paid particular attention to the 'sitty' trees they favour. Only then have I started to trap in earnest. When the Larsen traps are catching well, I have removed one squawking crow after another and have smiled a time or two when dispatching them. The smile has been raised in connection with the official guideline's sanctimonious instruction that the trapped bird should be killed out of sight of the call bird. I have always favoured a work glove for handling trapped crows or call birds as they have a painful peck, which teaches you all you need to know about the fatal damage they are capable of inflicting on a clutch of eggs, chicks and nestlings.

The magpie has nothing like the weight and power of the crow. He makes up for this by having even better eyesight, and is of course lethal to small and ground nesting birds. It's my belief the magpie is more readily caught in the Larsen trap than the crow, and the numbers that can be caught during a spring campaign makes one wonder where they all come from.

I have had little success in shooting crows and magpies. They usually fly too high to come within range of a shotgun. However, a gamekeeper friend did well by locating the nests of crows in woods and concealing himself within shotgun range on the wood floor. Providing his camouflage was perfect and he kept statue still, he could fool crows that were doubtless preoccupied with other matters and, in this way, he had the double satisfaction of fooling these sharp, cunning birds and ridding his shoot of them and their progeny.

In contrast to the crow, rooks – in reasonable numbers – are the farmers' friends, with their predilection for wire worm and grubs. Without doubt the most effective way to control rook populations is by holding the now unfashionable rook shoots. These require a small team of guns to visit the rookery in the course of a mid-May evening to shoot the young rooks perching on the branches in the vicinity of their nests. I believe the traditional date for this shoot was 13 May but, in the event of an earlier hatch, that may now be too

late. Rather than being driven by tradition, someone involved needs to keep an eye on the rate of growth of the young birds and the extent to which they are getting their wings.

It has not been my intention in this chapter to review the working life of a gamekeeper. Many authors have attempted that. However, I would say that the shooting man who simply shoots without any idea of the gamekeeper's regime misses a great deal of interest. If the shoot is a good one, with an adequate supply of game that meets his expectations and is well presented, his pleasure would be enhanced if he knew how this had been achieved. If he is involved in a failing shoot, an understanding of what is or what is not going on in his absence might assist him in deciding if the shoot can be improved or if there is no hope of that happening.

I was fortunate in that I grew up around gamekeepers and picked up some knowledge of their profession from them, which provided a foundation for me in my own various amateur gamekeeper assignments. In my early 30s, I was working very long hours as a solicitor and needed an antidote to my confinement in an office. Through a friend who was in a similar position, I became involved with a small farmers' shoot. The farmer owner of Cocks Farm Shoot had a great asset in his land, which was perfect for shooting. The geography of the place was like one of those innumerable sketches of perfect shoots I drew secretly during boring lessons at school. There was a stream and a lake and a marshy area. There were rough water meadows and arable land. There were several copses, spinneys, and woods, with ponds here and there.

During the spring and summer my friend and I used to kill some vermin and try to improve the cover in some of the neglected belts and copses. Then, from the arrival of the poults, which went into a central release pen, we would feed our separate beats. I usually fed mine late at night after work and came to know my woods and belts very well from walking through them in the dark. We ran the shoot days and had some interesting times trying to present the best possible birds, particularly from the outlying belts and copses, as there were no game covers on the farm at all.

My friend and I helped out the owner of this shoot for several years, recieving grateful thanks from the owner for our efforts and the excellent days we put on for him. We derived some satisfaction from showing his game in some sporting drives. Unfortunately, he had as a shooting partner a coarse chap who spoiled it all. From this experience, I made a golden rule, which I have adhered to ever since. It is that a successful pheasant shoot must have both good politics and good geography.

While anyone could have held his pheasants on Cocks Farm Shoot, so good was the layout and, in particular, the warm wet reed beds in the middle of the shoot, the opposite was true of Highgrave Farm. A postage stamp of a place, with three cold, neglected woods on the top of a hill for cover, I could and did envisage every season of my involvement culminating in situations where all the poults on the farm walked down the hill and across the road, never to return. I had nightmares about it, and never more than when there was a dry autumn. There was an amateur gamekeeper there, an old soldier of decided character. He was the first to admit he did not know a great deal about being a gamekeeper, but he was extremely conscientious. He never missed a feed and kept his numerous hoppers filled and every water trough full, and there was one of these containers for every feeder on the shoot. With specialist help in killing visiting foxes, this old soldier held the pheasants throughout the season in these most unpromising of situations. Returns of pheasants shot were in the order of between 50 and 60 percent of pheasants released. These were incredibly strong returns, which put many a professional gamekeeper to shame and showed what could be achieved through hard, regular work on a shoot. These stunning results reminded me of the sensational shooting my father generated from his reliable stewardship of three feed rides in a vicarage shrubbery.

opposite:
Shooting harvest

Fun With Ferrets

There are shooting men who restrict themselves to big days. When it comes to shooting, they do not get out of bed for less than a bag of several hundred and a day's entertainment which perhaps includes a gourmet lunch and fine wines. Although some do, I personally do not in any way deplore these participants. They pay the wages of a great many gamekeepers and, by their lavish expenditure, bring other income into rural areas and the shooting industry. As I do not think it wrong to shoot pheasants, I do not row along with the puritanical argument, not infrequently rehearsed, that it is fine to shoot five of them but not 50 or 500 or some other number. The difficulty I have with such characters is not what they do at all, but what they do not. Many of these sadly deprived big guns have no notion of the opportunities provided by lesser sport in shooting. They have never flighted wigeon under the moon or waited, at dusk, for teal by a splash. Business and other affairs of state will have precluded them from snatching by-days and forays with friends and dogs with a shared love of shooting. I have these moguls tagged as men who have never had any fun with ferrets.

Like many boys in my time, I had my own ferret. 'Minnie' was an albino jill ferret, supplied to me as a kit by a local gamekeeper. Initially, I was scared of her – frightened that she would bite me – but when I found she did not, I began handling her with increasing confidence. Very soon, my ferret and I were inseparable, and I would carry her around under my shirt. My ferret was not the most popular member of the Vicarage establishment, particularly when she 'got in' with my sister's guinea pig. How she gained access to the guinea pig pen remains shrouded in mystery.

Much later, I took up ferreting and kept an albino hob and jill named Sonny and Cher. After my childhood experience of keeping a jill ferret in a cage, and discovering that she was a princess of escapology, I designed and had made by a joiner a robust square metre pen, the heavy top lid of which was the only opening. The use of light weld mesh all round defeated Sonny and Cher's best efforts to scratch their way out through the sides of this pen and, in several years, there was never a successful break-out from it. Inside the pen I placed miscellaneous items such as plastic tubes and drainage pipes, and climbing frames. These gave Sonny and Cher full scope to enjoy life when they were not out rabbiting and the exercise kept them in the pink.

I had some fun days ferreting with these two miscreants, and enjoyed several humorous incidents.

At that time the local gamekeeper's father, Pop, lived in the village and was very keen and an expert on ferreting. He was a retired coal miner from Mansfield and had been, like so many miners, keen on country sports. In other words, he had

been an inveterate poacher. A master of the shaggy ferret story, he had a nicely turned tale about a ferreting outing that he and his mate, Horace, had made. As rabbits in the Mansfield locality were in short supply, no doubt at least partially due to the depredations of Pop and Horace, the two of them decided to drive to the Lincolnshire coast where they hoped to have some first class sport. They put their equipment and a box of ferrets in Horace's ancient van and headed off as night was falling. A few miles out of the mining district, they came across a freshly run over, clean rabbit in the road. They stopped the van, picked up the rabbit and put it in the back of the van. When they reached the coast things did not go as planned at all. It was a pitch black night and they couldn't find the warrens they had come to ferret. After midnight it started to rain heavily, and in the early hours they drove back towards Mansfield comprehensively defeated. As they approached their homes, they had a minor argument as to which of them should have the roadkill rabbit, all they had to show for their night's work. Horace won, or thought he had, until they opened the back door of the van and discovered that the ferrets had escaped their box and eaten the rabbit.

When digging was required while ferreting, Pop had a distinctive style unlike anything I had previously seen. He would sit down and shovel out earth as easily as if it was soap powder. He achieved this by upper body strength alone, using his hugely strong shoulders, no doubt acquired over years of practice down in the mine. He had good concentration out ferreting and became irritated by anyone there not paying full attention. A friend of mine came one morning to see how the job was done. Rabbits were slow to bolt and my friend fidgeted. At length, he announced he had to be going and Pop, looking up briefly from the hole over which he had his ear cocked, responded tartly by saying that was the most useful thing he had done all morning.

I enjoyed occasional days spent ferreting in February with Pop's son. We went one morning to the wood adjacent to my cottage. There, the bank around the edge of the wood was home to a good population of rabbits. With two of us we progressed efficiently up the south side of the wood. We used e-collars on the ferrets and carried ferret finders. We gave the ferrets a few minutes in each hole and if the rabbit did not bolt and the ferret did not show itself then one of us went forward and located it. I used a sharp, narrow rabbiting spade and

that made for easy digging. On the top of the day, we sat on a log in the sunshine and ate our pieces. The gamekeeper referred to this as his bun and told me that when he wrote his memoirs he would entitle them: "When I Ate My Bun." He invariably kept his gun beside him in the hope that some vermin bird or animal would pass within range.

One early February day I was invited to ferret the rabbits on a farm a few miles from my home. The rabbit burrows were in a light land belt called Fourteen Acre. It was a long straight belt that started on the top of the hill at the east end and ran due west down that hill and up the one on the other side. There was a passable track on the north side of it. I was on my own that day, and it was a cracking day to be rabbiting, with a pale sunshine after frost and a rising breeze throughout the day. I shot a rabbit from the first hole and from then on the ferrets were either bolting or holing up rabbits all day. The digging was easy, and once I found my little jill lying up with two rabbits. As usual, I put my boot in the hole while I pulled a rabbit out by his back legs and, on taking a second look, I could see the blue-grey back of the other one, which I also extracted.

I emptied the bladder of each rabbit I accounted for and hurdled it. Then, I hung it on a convenient branch and continued to work my way along the belt. Late in the morning, a young girl walked by with

above:
A good bag of rabbits

a Labrador. She was the owner's pretty daughter and was not at all upset by the rabbits hanging at intervals alongside the track. By three o'clock in the afternoon, I had reached the west end of the belt and had killed 15 rabbits. That was a record for me, and I decided to finish my day with a pigeon roost shoot in the wood called Lousy Bush. By the time I had collected the rabbits and put up the ferrets, the afternoon was getting on and the first pigeons were hammering into the teeth of the now near gale force wind for shelter. I had an hour's great sport there and finished with a pigeon pick up just in double figures.

Driving home with the truck full of rabbits, pigeons, ferrets and equipment I thought I was the luckiest man in England. I had succeeded beyond measure in that most testing of challenges: making a great day's shooting sport in February. Years later, should I ever be tempted to lounge around the house in early February, I revisit that mixed day's ferreting and pigeon flighting to remind myself what can be done if you get out there and do it.

Another ferreting assignment came my way in ironic circumstances. In the course of my professional practice, I had dealings with a land agent who, at that time, acted for the Nature Conservancy Council, as it was then. He and I had a difficult and protracted negotiation, in the course of which we got to know each other quite well and had established a good rapport. One day, he took me to one side and asked if I would assist him with a delicate problem. He was responsible, he told me, for a conservation project involving the re-introduction of rabbits to the historic Brettenham Heath Warren. Now of course I knew of the Brettenham Warren by reputation. Its productivity and the work of the warreners there were mainly over before my time, but were part of local folklore and legend in the Breck. I once visited the Rought-Roughts' rabbit skin factory in Brandon and briefly met Lionel. I recall inspecting a bundle of dried rabbit skins on the factory floor. Although I knew the history, I had no idea that the NCC was re-introducing rabbits in the expectation that when they cropped the grass certain unusual wild flowers – flora particular to the Breck – would flourish again. The land agent explained that I was not on any account to kill these rabbits, which had apparently been caught up in live catch traps and transported from the Suffolk coast at great expense. No, his problem was that some of these rabbits had burrowed underneath the rabbit netting around the warren and taken up residence in an ancient thorn belt outside the warren and adjacent to a tenant farmer's arable field. I was to only ferret the rabbits in the thorn belt and I was, he said, the only man he would entrust with the task, the temptations of ferreting the warren itself being so strong.

That was how, one Sunday morning, I found myself on the edge of Brettenham Warren with my friend, Sampson. Once outside the rabbit netting that separated the warren from the thorn belt, we took stock of the scene. There were holes a-plenty, but most of these were between the roots of the gnarled old thorn trees and bushes, the main roots and trunks of which were of impressive diameter. The holes had that long-used look about them that indicated they would not be easy to ferret. Anyway, we entered a ferret in a hole at one end of the belt and Sampson shot a rabbit that bolted, and then another. This good start slowed up when the ferret got laid up with a rabbit, and I had to start digging. I found the soil to be comprised of a fine, soft sand, and the holes to be really deep. Further, the holes ran around the great roots of the thorns, which were mainly far too well established to cut or break. I used a shovel rather than a spade, and removed a good heap of sand from the hole and then needed to put my head and body into the excavation to recover the ferret and rabbit. With Sampson holding onto my ankles, I lowered myself gingerly down the excavated pit, with a trickle of sand following me. To say the least, I was terrified of a cave-in as I could see myself being buried upside down if the sides of the hole collapsed. As quickly as I could, I grabbed the ferret and rabbit and shouted to Sampson to get me out of there.

The morning went on in that way. When a rabbit bolted, there was little top cover to conceal it and Sampson did good work with his gun. However, rabbits were sticky, and every rabbit hole seemed to be four of five feet deep. By the time we had finished, our bag was disappointing considering the amount of rabbit work in and around the thorn belt, but we left with a feeling of some relief. Our day's ferreting had been downright dangerous and, whenever I drive by now, I think ruefully how I might quite easily have been buried in a bury on Brettenham Heath.

Another distinctive character with whom I passed a day or two's ferreting was a builder called Mac. He can vouch for a most unusual ferreting moment. We were ferreting in the edge of some old cattle meadows. These were typical, traditional cattle meadows with a small stream running through them and a long, scrubby belt of trees the length of the north side. This belt held a few rabbits and I used to ferret it once a year after the end of the game shooting season. In truth, it was an awkward place to ferret with a lot of bramble patches, and dangerous pieces of barbed wire fencing, the legacy of the efforts of various long gone graziers to keep their steers in the meadows.

On the afternoon of the incident, I came on a good-sized, fresh rabbit hole just inside the barbed wire. Entering the ferret, I did not trouble to clamber over the wire again but stood back a couple of yards into the belt ready for a shot with my single barrel 12-bore Baikal which, at that time, was my usual ferreting gun. In as long as it takes to write this, a monster dog fox bolted and made to cross the grass. I gave no quarter and rolled him over before he had gone five yards. Then, Sonny, my big white hob ferret, appeared at the entrance to the hole none the worse for his encounter.

As the usual outcome of such an underground encounter is a dead ferret, I was amazed that my ferret had not only bolted a fox, but such a big one. Mac the builder was well impressed too, and often referred to the affair when we shot together afterwards. I liked Mac and, having observed his love of shooting, invited him to shoot several times. We had some fun times.

In the course of my ferreting, I had some encounters which, in hindsight, were amusing. I helped one farmer throughout the game shooting season on the understanding that I would have the rabbiting in February. I called him to arrange the days and he mentioned that he had borrowed a ferret and just let it "run through a few holes". The next season he let a passing gipsy ferret the best hedges, and – although a slow learner – I had at last learned enough about him not to ferret

opposite:
Ready to go

above:
A likely hole

spoiled as a youngster, but nothing could excuse the way he spoke to his gamekeeper, beaters, and even his guest guns. One Sunday morning after the end of the game shooting season I was ferreting a bank at the invitation of his gamekeeper. 'Mr Spoilt Brat' appeared in an adjoining field of rough cover with dog and gun and started shouting and making a demonstration. To start with I thought he was shouting at his dog, but then I realised he was shouting at me. Perhaps sensibly, he did not approach me.

One day my lad was beating on his shoot and had my old lab with him in an early season drive out of a field of sugar beet. Just before the end of the drive, with guns and beaters close together, Mr Spoilt Brat engaged a helicopter of a cock pheasant with a close range shot. My old dog trotted forward a few yards and picked the bird, upon which that man went up to the dog and kicked him as hard as he could under the chin. It was a drop kick. I was not informed of this until some years afterwards and have never seen that man since the incident came to my knowledge. That's probably a good thing. This fellow got his just desserts in the end when, tired of his tantrums, not even his friends would shoot with him any longer, and he had to resort to selling his second rate days to keep his shoot going. He was such a petulant fellow that he was best suited to shooting on his own.

there again. Inevitably, he called me the following February to ask when I was going to bring my ferrets over and "kill the damn rabbits."

Another landowner I gave up on was a petulant chap, whose moods changed with the wind. No doubt he had been

Another farmer I used to ferret for was aware of my being "the son of the manse", as they say in Scotland. He found great amusement in my practice of ferreting on Sundays and, on greeting me, invariably enquired whether the rabbits had bolted well on the previous Sunday morning.

Another, rather grand landowner was having trouble with rabbits in his fine country house garden and asked if I would attend with the ferrets. He told me the old, retired keeper would show me the holes. I duly appeared and met old Johnny – a well-known local gamekeeper and a character – who led me into a beautiful flower garden in front of the

'big house'. My efforts that morning were unsuccessful as the burrows were not tenanted. However, I kept trying and at the last hole netted a big, old doe rabbit, which was not far short of giving birth to a litter of several youngsters. Johnny and I settled for that and, as we walked past the garden shed, he nipped inside and came out with two bottles of fine old vintage claret. "Here," he said, handing one to me and stowing the other in the poacher's pocket of his tweed coat, "His Lordship said I was to give you that if you got several rabbits, and with the doe and youngsters we can call it seven, so that's one bottle for you and one for me!"

above left:
Entering the ferret

above right:
Nothing at home

Days at the Grouse

As we negotiated the broken ground at the north end of Loch Skerray, my godson young Anthony was on the right, closest to the loch. He was carrying a 20-bore, as he had been doing all week, and up to that point had not accounted for a grouse. We – his father, his feisty mother, young Anthony and I – were in the process of wheeling right round the end of the loch to take a sweep back up the ridge. In front of us the English setter, Ivy, quartered in her quiet manner, and none of us thought the prospect of flushing grouse was high. The long walk in the heat and the heather had taken its toll and our optimism was at a low ebb.

Then, Ivy had a set. I saw her in the peat hags, her head stretched forward, her flag stretched back. Motionless, she was taut with life and the scent of grouse. Signalling to Anthony to get ready, I walked forward and, stroking her forward by her collar, flushed the pair. The hen went forward low, unshot at, but the cock grouse turned and climbed high over the loch presenting Anthony with a beautiful driven shot which he judged to perfection. The grouse crumpled and splashed down into the loch. My Labrador retrieved the bird and I handed it to my godson. He had walked all week, in wet and dry. He had tramped the moors where, at times, grouse seemed to be rarer than hens' teeth. He had had chances and missed them. At last, he held his first grouse, and in a perfect place

where the heather of the hill and the water in the loch met under the shimmering late afternoon heat haze. I was so pleased for him; I walked a little way away to allow him a few moments to embed a shooting experience he will never forget. I shuffled off a few yards and made a fuss of the dogs. "Well done, Anthony!" shouted his mother, "Good shot! Good shot!" With those words, she broke the spell and, reloading, I clicked the setter into action again.

For some years I took a week or a fortnight's grouse shooting on the Tongue estate in north Sutherland. I believe the estate was about 10,000 acres in extent, and the terrain varied considerably. Above Brae Tongue, there was some high, steep ground which, if little else, gave superlative views out to sea to the north, for the estate was right on the north coast. Then, there were areas around the River Borgie, where the ground was quite rugged although not as high as that first described. Further north the ground was more representative of the flow country, with many acres of flat, wet ground, which was interspersed with lochs and bogs. Nearer the coast, the ground was rockier.

There were grouse on most of this ground, although nowhere in very great numbers, and in some places they were downright scarce. We discovered, and we had to work this out for ourselves, that the hill close to the sea was unproductive because of the depredation of the gulls. The boggy

above:
Grouse retrieved

flow country was not much favoured. The highest ground usually housed barren pairs of displaced old birds. On the best banks, where the bonny heather was, there we would find coveys.

The estate was unkeepered, so vermin control was non-existent unless foxes were bothering the flocks at lambing time. The local crofters set fire to the hill at will and I remember the bonny heather in the best area that we saw on our first visit had all been destroyed by fire before we returned the next year. That fire was said to be accidental. The weather on the north coast can be very bad, and this was another factor that the local grouse had to contend with in their fight for survival.

The result of these problems was that coveys were often few in number and size. Our record day was six brace, and on most visits we had a bag of five brace once in eight or 10 days of shooting. We rarely experienced a blank day, but often came off the hill with only two or three brace to show for our day's walking.

We never used a full team of bird dogs but relied either on our own Labradors or, more often, a bird dog that we used to hire from the admirable Mrs Campbell of Bower in Caithness. I first heard about the legendary Mrs Campbell and her setter and pointer kennels during one of my early annual visits, and wrote to her in the winter saying I understood she had dogs to hire, and enquiring whether she had one available for me for the first two weeks of the following September. In due course, I received Mrs Campbell's reply. She informed me that she had 'a suitable animal' for me. So it was that, having travelled to the north coast on the Saturday, I drove across to Bower on the Sunday morning and took temporary possession of a fine-looking but extremely dirty red setter called Bracken. I stopped in Thurso on the way back to our holiday cottage and bought some dog shampoo, which I applied liberally while bathing Bracken in a roadside loch. I then introduced him to my wife and children who spent much time grooming him, all of which he took in good part. He was a good-natured old dog.

On the Monday, it was a very smart-looking setter that we took to the hill. Having shot over setters years before I was optimistic, but my old companion, Adrian, and my young son, Toby, were highly sceptical as to the outcome. Happily, their doubts were soon to be dispelled. As soon as we were ready Bracken was cast off and soon found the only pace he knew, which was, in equine language, a steady canter. While we plodded through the heather, Bracken quartered tirelessly over a front of around 600 yards. We guns soon dropped into the easy routine of it in that marvellous armed walk over the hills, with the comfortable southerly breeze and the soft early autumn sun in our faces. We strolled while Bracken ran, and in the haze and the heat he became like a metronome, endlessly crossing and re-crossing in front of us.

And then he was not crossing, not there. But he was there, motionless in a rank heather dell holding grouse. As we moved up and made ready, the old dog swivelled his eyes as if to tell us that we should hurry, as it was no easy business holding the agitated covey. All this time he stood set – stiff legged, focused and concentrating – absolute master of the birds. The covey jumped; there was a ragged volley of shots and, here and there, a grouse down. While we searched for them, Bracken found a wet sphagnum-mossed hole and submerged himself in it to emerge looking more skeletal than ever. His legs were long and for running, his chest for the containment of his massive lungs, and his long nose was the receptacle for the scents of grouse. He really was a master of his craft.

In the days that followed, unless it was raining, we went to the hill with Bracken. At the start of the day, with Bracken still on the leash, he would take in great gulps of air and scent off the hills and quiver beneath his fine red coat. Then, as soon as he was unrestrained, he would pick up speed and run and run for the sheer joy of grouse hunting. Although those days are distant now, my mind's eye still sees him crossing and re-crossing the heather shoulders above the river, a dog of most noble appearance and mien. We walked behind him while he worked for us and always, when he held the birds, he succeeded in appearing most contemptuous of us and our abilities with the gun as, while invariably biting his long lips, he simultaneously overlooked the grouse and looked back at us, in so doing urging us to hurry to the set.

One day, I took an English doctor out with me. He had shot grouse over dogs many years before on the north-east coast of Scotland. He told me the grouse had been plentiful there, but that the week had become too expensive. The doctor and I worked a cheek wind along the north-west side of Loch Craggie, where the slopes were steep and fluted in shape. Here and there, there were good coveys and we put up one with 15 grouse in it. None of the coveys we encountered nearer the coast were so large. The doctor shot straight that morning. When we stopped for our piece Bracken threw himself down for a well-earned rest. My piece was, as usual, all protein – ham and dried fruit – but the doctor produced

above:
Drive's end

some sandwiches from his pocket, which can make a man wickedly thirsty.

I remember how we lay back comfortably, resting our backs on the slope of the hill side, and that we overlooked Loch Craggie and a long length of Loch Loyal and then, far above, the great mass of Ben Loyal and the lesser but still impressive ridges of Ben Stumahadh. We talked in a companionable manner and he told me an unusual war story. At his public school during the early and middle years of the war, he had become accustomed to the frequent announcements of the deaths of old boys who had been known to him. By the time he was old enough to join up, he said he and his contemporaries expected that they too

would be killed. After basic training, he had been one of a draft of battle replacement casualties on a troop ship in the Channel when the war ended. After so lengthy a preparation, he had experienced mixed feelings about the cessation of hostilities, which were only partially lessened by service immediately afterwards in Greece during its dreadful civil war.

Other guest guns included a brace of nephews and one of their contemporaries. They came up in the first season that I took the shooting. All three of them shot their first grouse with me, except my youngest nephew, Ben, who was not allowed to count his. What happened was that we had a day on the highest ground on the estate, and were walking and having the occasional shot up at 1,000 feet or thereabouts. At some distant point in the outward leg, young Ben had his chance and shot his first grouse. He proudly fastened this to his belt and walked with us for the rest of the day. When we reached the vehicles, foot sore and aching after a long, hard day, we laid out the bag, such as it was, and Ben discovered to his disappointment that his grouse had fallen off his belt and was lost somewhere on the illimitable hill. His disappointment was then grievously aggravated by his brother and chum, both adjudicating that as the grouse was not in the bag it could not be counted by Ben as his first grouse. His howls of frustrated rage were ignored and from that day to this his brothers have never been slow to retell the story of the first grouse that wasn't. I suspect Ben made good the loss during the remaining days he was with me, but such was the scarcity of stock that every bird bagged or missed, as the case was, had an excitement and satisfaction value that would be unthinkable on any well-stocked grouse moor.

Not all my guests appreciated the hard work required to make a bag of grouse on the Tongue estate. I mean they didn't like the distance between each one. Before one season, I was told by a mutual friend that a wealthy man and his family, which included a teenaged son, would be staying in a local lodge. It seemed they had taken the fishing on the River Borgie for the week and wanted some grouse shooting to supplement that sport. Rather against my better judgement, I agreed to take the boy out with me and made what plans I could to show him some sport. However, early contact suggested I was being used to 'entertain' the lad, and I use that word advisedly, as I didn't sense any real sporting enthusiasm. It was not made clear to me what experience the boy had with a shotgun. Anyway, I decided to take him out one afternoon and work a beat into the wind. There was a heather ridge there that sometimes held grouse. That afternoon, we walked a few yards to the highest point of this, where there was a bowl-shaped area. Here, in an area the size of a tennis court, we flushed and shot two grouse. Then three rose and were also accounted for and then, I think, a single bird not far off. "That's the way to do it," observed the elder brother, "We have shot the whole family without walking a yard!"

I think the lad felt he had done grouse shooting that afternoon, and did not ask me for another outing. If he has ever shot grouse again it will doubtless have been on some well-keepered driven moor. I blamed his father for failing to embed in him any notion of the fun and pleasure involved in being a sportsman and a sporting shooter.

Another visitor was John, who was at that time a fit rugby-playing forester, and who was, and is, a delightful man. I

mention his fitness because it turned out it was a good thing he was, because of a small mistake he made one day on the hill. That day, with a north wind, we left John's car near the coast, at the north end of the estate, and took John in my truck as far as we could to the south. This was to give us a full day's dogging up into the wind and would, we planned, give us maximum sport without any dreaded downwind reaches. Having left my truck and walked northwards for an hour we took a break, which was when John discovered he had left the keys to his car in the pocket of his fleece in my truck. There was nothing for it but for him to leg it back to the truck and pick up the keys. His distance from them was only going to increase if we kept going. My other companion and I each selected one those comfortable resting places; half short, dry heather and half smooth, sloping rock, with which north Sutherland is so well supplied, and waited on John's return. I think he must have run there and back because, after an incredibly short space of time, he re-appeared over the ridge with his car keys raring to chase some more grouse. John was the right type for that sort of shooting and he, my friend Adrian, his son Anthony, and my own son made most memorable those happy, carefree days when we were at the grouse.

Our adventures in north Sutherland stoked my interest in rough grouse shooting and led me into other shooting.

One example of this was Lamb Hill near Strathaven in south-west Scotland. The leaseholder of Lamb Hill, a great character known throughout south and central Scotland as 'Greengrass', suggested I should shoot Lamb Hill. There were a few grouse there, he said.

The presence of any grouse there at all seemed unlikely to my small party as we debouched from our vehicles in the middle of a large area of commercial forestry. Our instructions were to stay and shoot within the forestry fence, and the many acres of spruce trees that blanketed the ground looked totally useless as grouse

above:
An upland harvest

cover. However, as we were there, we made ready and started to work our way upwards towards the top side of the forest by way of a wide heather ride, approaching 100 yards in width in places. Although we didn't see any grouse, we saw grouse foil, and continued the steep climb uphill with increasing hope. Eventually, emerging at the top of the trees, we walked out on to a proper heather moor, some of which at least was within the post and rail fence delineating the boundary of our ground. Soon after spreading out to walk this, we shot a brace of grouse from a respectable covey that got up, and saw another covey go away too soon. Later, hunting in one of the wide rides again, the dogs flushed a pair of old birds from rank heather and we added them to our bag. We came off the hill exhausted by the stiff climb and the difficult walking in the rank heather. However, we were well pleased with our small bag, which demonstrated the truth of Greengrass' assertion that there were grouse there.

On another visit, we had a young man with us who had never previously shot a grouse. If he shot one, it would be a first. I stressed to him how unlikely it was that he would even see a grouse, let alone be in a position to get off a shot. With these caveats still ringing in his ears, we lined out on the track by the cars with the young man on the left flank. We had walked no more than 10 yards when a single grouse jumped out of the heather and crossed just in front of him. It was an easy shot and he made no mistake. That was his first grouse, shot within a minute of his first grouse hunt. On Lamb Hill that day he did not bag another.

For many years I had invited my old friend, Trembler, to join our party dogging up grouse in Sutherland. He would never come, but my stories about our small forays must have kindled some interest because one autumn Trembler and our mutual friend, Agriman, arranged two days of rough grouse shooting in Angus and very generously invited me to join them. I accepted without hesitation. As it happened, I was seeking to buy a German shorthaired pointer bitch at that time and had one on approval, which I was most anxious to test on the hill.

That was how it came about that on the appointed September day, Trembler, Agriman, and I began our day's walking up in the rolling braes, where I noticed the moorland landscape was a deal softer than that of Sutherland, and the areas of heather much more extensive. There were grouse there all right, and soon we were encountering coveys and pairs of them. Agriman was having a lucky day and was in the shooting. With some assistance from my Welsh pointer bitch, I also had plenty of sport. Agriman and I were busy all morning compiling the bag which, entirely by chance, left poor Trembler – who was

paying for this very expensive day – without a grouse to his name. We stopped for a piece on the hillside from which we could see way down the glen into the fertile agricultural plain of arable Angus and to Kirremuir. It was a grand view and all the better for the good company of my two companions. After we re-started, we hoped Trembler's luck would change, but it was not to be. It was just one of those days when he was destined to be out of the shooting. We came to the end of our walk on the main moor and were left with a thin strip of bonny heather. The keeper recommended Trembler walk through the middle of it and that I go on his left. Agriman unloaded and walked behind us. Inevitably, the only grouse in the strip flushed at my feet in such a way that Trembler could not engage them. We finished that day with the impressive total of 12 brace, double the number I had ever had in Sutherland.

On the next day, we went to Glen Shee to try for ptarmigan and grouse.

We walked the high hill there, our route taking us through the various paling fences that contained the ski routes in winter. Trembler had insisted on bringing his cannon – a cumbersome over-and-under 12-bore better suited to a trap range than the hill – and I watched with cruel amusement as the barrels of this became temporarily blocked with sphagnum moss as he sought to crawl under the fence. We found a few ptarmigan and grouse on the tops. Then the young keeper and his team put in a couple of impromptu drives. By the time we stood for the second of these, the wind had risen to near gale force and it was obvious that any grouse coming forward would be really travelling downwind very fast indeed.

We saw and shot at some superb driven grouse in the next few minutes. I was at the bottom of the gun line when at last my turn came with a high, fast screamer that, receiving the full pattern of shot, fell a full 150 yards behind me. At my shot, the Welsh pointer bitch was gone in hot pursuit, and by the time I reached her, all that was left of my grouse was one solitary, heavily feathered claw. As if that was not enough to guarantee her a return ticket to Wales, that evening she jumped up six or seven feet to steal and eat a brace of the grouse shot the previous day, which was hanging on the wall outside her kennel.

That day on Glen Shee was another cracking one, and I was somewhat apprehensive as to whether my friends would enjoy the more specialist pleasures of Lamb Hill, which I had invited them to sample with me on the way south. By the time we arrived there it was the middle of an uncomfortably warm autumn morning, but this didn't prevent Trembler from dressing up in his full shooting suit. I think he regretted that as by the time we emerged on to the moor at the top of the trees, he was really cooked, and looked it. Fortunately, he shot a grouse that rose and flew back over him, actually falling in the spruce trees below him. Later on, we jumped some duck and, with all of us having had a shot or two, left that place.

In another season, I took a day's walked up grouse shooting on Lowther Estate's Shap Fell. Shap is an island moor on the edge of the Lake District hills with the old road marking the boundary between these and the Pennines to the east. I believe it is this that accounts for Shap's bad weather, which I have experienced more than once. However, on that day the weather was temperate and the grouse plentiful. Under the supervision of the highly professional grouse moor keeper, John Carr, we made a good bag.

However, my personal view was, and is, that walked up grouse shooting, even on productive moors, did not generate the same excitement as did shooting grouse over setter and pointer dogs. The 'dogging up' of grouse drew out of me and my companions an atavistic satisfaction that was lacking when the grouse were flushed by busy spaniels or kicked out of the heather. I came to the conclusion that if I was not able to experience the emotionally charged moments that only occur while shooting over dogs, then the next best way of shooting grouse was when they were driven towards you.

Over several years, I have been very fortunate to receive invitations to shoot over the Ministry of Defence moors at Warcop, and to enjoy wonderful days with the syndicates that run them. The grouse days on both Hilton and the smaller Warcop moor are long, hard days on the hill. With four drives, each having no less than 17 butts, each of the teams walk two and stand two drives during the course of the day. At Warcop, the walk back to the vehicles by all the guns is a bonus manoeuvre, and frequently the most productive one of that day. Although the walking guns can shoot and, indeed, often get more shooting than the standing guns, it's the chance of a driven bird over my butt that keeps my fires alight through the long, hard days there.

One memorable November day, I was a guest on a late season Warcop day. The word was that there were still plenty of grouse there. When we met in the morning, I was allocated to the Black team, which meant I would be walking in drives one and three and standing in drives two and four. It's difficult to decide what kit to take on a Warcop day, as there is no question of slipping back to your truck for a change of coat or whatever. Whatever you need for the day you must take with you. I made final adjustments to my load, and managed to get all I wanted into a day sac, and so avoided taking a full rucksack.

There was a long walk to the start point for the first drive, but I was expecting this, and kept up with the young chaps in my team. On reaching the knoll we took a breather before our team leader briefed us on the dos and don'ts of the day, and instructed us to dress from the centre and keep in line. He then indicated our start points, with mine being only two guns from where we were. I walked down there with old Brandy and found I was to wait in a wet, boggy patch. At length we started and very soon I had a shot and a kill. That was a good start and, after Brandy had made the retrieve, I stowed my grouse in my day sac. The second drive saw me standing by the bank of a burn looking up the slope in front of me. There was a distinct swale in front of my butt, which I felt might channel grouse towards me. As it was, my first chance was at one of a covey that skidded from left to right. I dropped the first bird and missed the second. Then I had a singleton flying the same route but closer. I picked him off the end of the gun barrels and saw him down in a fluster of feathers. One more, this time coming straight at me down the

opposite:
Butt 5: a good drive

swale – a shot I fluff more often than not – and the drive was done.

I put my unloaded gun down and went out to pick up. As so often happens, the ground where the birds had come to rest looked quite different, and for some while I couldn't find any of them. Then, I stumbled on one and Brandy picked another. Going back towards the butt, he then found the third – the last one – in rank heather.

It had been a great morning for me, and it was now time to enjoy my piece.

The third drive had me in some big country, and I accounted for one more grouse just over the hill I had to climb, and Brandy retrieved another that my neighbour shot, which fell into a rocky burn. When we walk the local rule is that we only shoot one bird, as otherwise the line gets too long delayed. I reminded myself of this rule as the coveys went forward as one before I shot a right and left. Happily, I was then able to pick both birds quite quickly so no harm was done. On this afternoon, I came up to the gun line at the butt occupied by my host. He had had a good drive, and Brandy and I helped him pick up as quickly as possible before he had to walk out to the back of the return drive with the rest of the Red team. They did a good job and, standing on the edge of the biggest burn on the moor, I had some classy driven shooting, accounting for another three grouse. In this drive, the grouse flying forward have to fly over

a wide valley with steeply rising ground immediately behind the butts. This means the standing guns get plenty of notice that the grouse are on the wing and mine were high, fast fliers. That was four brace for me and there was still the long walk home. I turned round and took a line directly behind me while some of the local experts made their way down to the left-hand side of the line to nail the grouse that they anticipated would go that way. By now there was a stiff breeze in our faces and, with grouse wanting to get back to their own territories, there were a good number of them coming back like driven birds over the line. I was particularly lucky with three high, fast grouse dead and down so that Brandy could retrieve them quickly and without any fuss. Then, I had a really long crosser to complete my bag of six brace for that most memorable of days.

My recollections of it are all the sweeter for having shot straight, and I have less happy memories of two other days at the grouse when I shot really badly. On the first of these, when I was at university, I walked with my host, a man who I believe became one of the best grouse shots in England. Even as a very young man his shooting was lethal to the walked up grouse, whereas I missed and missed all day long. My only grouse down was a runner, which we could not find. We finished with an impromptu drive by the keeper and, although I had several chances, I just could not connect. That was during the time of my life when I could not even hit pheasants, so I had no hope at the grouse.

More recently, I was the right-hand gun in a line of walking guns, working into a stiff breeze. The other guns had some great shooting as the grouse curled and came back over the line. My position, near the top of a sloping moor, only afforded me going away chances at extreme range and I never picked up a grouse during the whole operation. How I would have loved to have been at the other end of the line!

The ultimate driven grouse shooting experience must surely be a day on Wemmergil Moor, and I am privileged to say I have enjoyed just that. Shooting there in September 2007, I had, as you would expect, the chance to get off plenty of shots. However, I had a problem all day and that was caused by my inherent reluctance to shoot low in front. Even if the beaters were miles away, I didn't like to do it. If there was a flanker I flinched from a shot in front and to the left or right depending on whether I was the gun on the left- or right-hand end of the line.

I shot the grouse quite well behind, and was glad and surprised to find at the end of the day that I had contributed my share of the bag. I only killed a few birds in front, and just couldn't get over the block that no doubt derived from all the conditioning I had received against low shooting in front all those years ago in my childhood.

My great day at Wemmergil should have been only the first half of the story of my driven grouse shooting experience, as my invitation extended to another day – the next day – at Stags Fell. Alas! The next morning, we awoke to a thick, immovable mist behind the hotel and although we hung about until mid-afternoon it never lifted, and not a shot was fired. That did for the second half of my driven grouse shooting career, and it was galling to drive out of the dales into bright late-afternoon sunshine under a clear blue sky.

I doubt I shall ever return to Wemmergil, or see packed grouse hurtling in their hundreds towards the butts. A day's shooting there was a great experience, and I can see how the devotees of it must regard it as the best of all the shooting sports. Although I would like to do it again, it is not imperative to me that I should do so. As far as I am concerned, I prefer to walk over the rolling moorland landscape of Sutherland with a keen companion and a steady setter. What does it for me is not guaranteed grouse in their thousands, but merely the chance of a shot. I love to plod across the illimitable moors and kick up the powdered heather pollen in the sunshine and against the breeze. I like nothing more than to watch the dog working wide, now on the skyline, then in a dell. The warmth of the day, the incomparable landscape, the high sky, the routine of the running dog, all these make the gun soporific. And then the dog is stopped, on point or set, and the game is on. Stalking up to the dog, the tension mounts to unbearable levels. The motionless dog, like a statue, holds the hidden grouse. Time stands still. And then the grouse flush and the guns shoot, and a grouse or two falls in a flurry of feathers. The spell is broken as the guns quietly pick up. They each know then they have experienced a moment in the deep, old heart of hunting.

Flight Time

My home county of Suffolk was, and is, predominantly dry. For this reason, my first taste of game shooting was with pheasants and partridges. However, I very soon experienced the most pleasurable pursuit of wildfowl, the enjoyment of which has never diminished for me one jot.

The first ducks I saw shot were mallard off a farmyard pond, and even as a youngster I understood this was an annual culling exercise to keep the pond's population of these feral ducks to a reasonable level. It was not intended to be a sporting drive, but was a job that needed doing when there were sufficient guns to surround the water.

In contrast, my youthful adventures in the local marsh known as the Wash are imprinted on my memory. The Wash comprised a mixed area of water meadow, rough grass, reeds and the like, either side of the headwaters of the River Stour. It was sufficiently large for a long morning's sport, and very exciting it was too. The river itself often afforded a chance at the mallard that frequented it. The drains and dykes that flowed into it were often good for teal. Occasionally, after heavy rain or snowfall, other duck would be drawn in by the flood water and then there might be a chance of wigeon. Once, on an adjacent field, I recall my father flooring a solitary goldeneye, a trophy bird in those parts.

Occasionally, an attempt would be made to drive snipe down the Wash. Invariably, by the time these small birds crossed the gun line they were a mile high. In any event most of them veered off the wash and made good their escape over the adjacent arable farmland. While my elders and betters grassed one or two, I did not succeed in shooting one at that time. However, while splashing around the wash, I formed an undying passion for shooting in wet, rushy places, and took much pleasure in learning to identify the different species of duck and waders and their collective names, such as a spring of teal and a wisp of snipe.

Some years later, my sister married a Norfolk farmer, a chap who was extremely knowledgeable about flight ponds and duck flighting. Dick Stanton farmed on the edge of the Wash at Dersingham in north-west Norfolk. For much of that time he owned a pond behind the sea wall much frequented by wigeon. He generously took me down there to flight on many occasions and these were outings I still cherish. His pond was a long one and on a south or north wind the guns were placed in hides on one side, usually facing west so that they had the benefit of the last of the evening light. Once in position, the guns waited for action. Often, I would watch the light being squeezed out of the sky with the colours of the day being replaced by sepia shades.

opposite:
Before a flight

above:
At the wild geese

There was much to see and hear. Often cock pheasants' heads would be silhouetted on the top of the sea wall as they made their way inland after a day foraging in the marram and the samphire on the seaward side of the bank. The evening curlew called and, on occasion, skeins of wild geese passed high overhead as they flew some miles inland to their night time feeding grounds.

Then, seemingly out of nowhere, would come the thrilling moment in which the wigeon came swirling and whistling into the pond. They would fling themselves downwards, these sky divers of the wildfowl world, and woe betide the gun who was not ready to shoot. As they passed in front, the waiting guns had to mount and swing in one movement and a duck or two would likely fall before the survivors rose up and away into the darkening sky. A few minutes further waiting and more wigeon would fly to the pond, and I can still see their dark shapes and hear their whistling there where the sea scent permeated the air.

Stanton taught me not to shoot a pond too late. His policy was to stop shooting while duck were still coming in to it. Apart from the conservationist effect of this limiting the bag, his forbearance was an investment in the next flight and ensured

trees in their attempts to escape, only to die of hypothermia during that long, tragic night.

At other times my brother-in-law instructed me in the management (for duck flighting) of a more modest farm pond. This was an old horse pond at the back of his farmyard, which typically was surrounded by blackthorn bushes except at its shallow end where, years before, the soil had been graded to make easy access for the heavy horses. The thorn was regularly cut back, with just enough growth being removed each year to allow the flighting duck easy access but not so much that the pond was open. I learned that it was vital for the pond to be a discreet one, where duck could rest and feed undisturbed.

His feeding regime was regular. He kept a rat-proof dustbin full of barley beside the pond and fed this grain into the shallow water on the pond margin. He fed into the water up to six or eight inches deep and did not feed on the land at all. Before every feed he would check whether the previous offering had been consumed. If there was still barley left in the shallow water, he would refrain from feeding at all.

The banks of the ponds had hides on them and as this small pond was generally shot by no more than two guns, it was possible to select the best hides for the prevailing wind on the night. If there

his pond would not become overshot and shot out.

I believe his sea wall pond was in fact a pit, that had been excavated to provide spoil for the sea wall that had been constructed after the 1953 floods. At that time there was a small settlement there on the edge of the Wash, unprotected by any sea defences. The infamous tidal surge was therefore unobstructed, and the wretched people who lived there attempted to flee across the farmland inland of their homes. Some – the lucky ones perhaps – were overwhelmed and drowned on the ground. Others took refuge in copses and woods, and climbed was no wind, there would be no flight. He regarded it as bad practice to disturb duck on a still evening.

Stanton kept a call duck on this pond. He favoured a single female mallard, which had a fox-free refuge on a small island in the middle of the pond. Her job was to entice passing drakes into visiting the pond. Whether it was her allure or the regular barley feed I do not know; whichever it was, the pond would routinely yield six or eight mallard duck in an evening flight.

Some years later, Stanton took me to a teal splash he had developed a couple of miles inland. This splash was close to a brook and was formed from a scrape made in the corner of a wet Norfolk reed bed. When first taken there, I observed signs of the similar, disciplined regime that I had seen on the farm pond. The barley bin was kept well filled. The hides were discreet and afforded the waiting guns good cover from view. No mallard or wigeon visited this little splash, but teal loved it.

On my first visit, Stanton explained that the teal would flight in so late that it would be usually impossible to intercept them on their way in. We would only see them when they were a few feet above the water. To overcome this late sighting he said that, as he saw the teal on the point of landing, he would discharge a

below:
Goose ambush

sacrificial shot into the air. This would cause the teal to flare up and provide shots as they hastily flew away. This clever ruse worked well and left two guns with the chance of three teal from each wisp that approached the pond, although this potential maximum was rarely achieved what with the failing light, small size of these lovely little duck, and the excitement of the moment.

Later on I was to acquire my own duck shoot in the East Anglian fens and had great fun with it. Mallard in particular bred prolifically in the fen drains, and in the September of a typical year numerous parties of these could be seen wheeling over the stubble fields. Careful reconnaissance was then needed to pick the correct part of the favoured field for a flight. As the fields had no cover in them, it was necessary to identify a suitably proximate dyke and hide in this. Occasionally, the dyke would be the right height so that the gun could stand in the bottom of it to see and shoot. More often, it would be far too deep and the gun would have to perch on one of the steep sides of the bank and take his shots from a position in which only a contortionist would have been comfortable. The mallard shot over the fenland stubbles were fine, fat birds and made superb eating.

After the stubbles had been ploughed, I turned my attentions to flighting on the river that formed the southern boundary of my shoot. Raised up between substantial banks, as fenland rivers usually are, the river was straight as far as the eye could see. 30 or 40 yards wide, it had well-reeded margins with, here and there, a stand of willow bushes. The pattern of an evening flight was set by the wind. What was ideally needed was a stiff upstream gale. The effect of this was to put a good wave on the surface water. On such evenings I would see the first mallard tracking back above the river heading for the lagoons and ponds that surrounded the sugar beet factory at Ely. On a still night, I could make out the duck turning their heads to inspect the river before they flew on. On a rough night, in contrast, the temptation was just too great. The duck would turn due east and lose height like so many aeroplanes coming in to land. Very often they would descend in a shallow trajectory and travel for hundreds of yards above the disturbed surface of the river.

Of these, many dropped in far short of my ambush position, but those that came on presented classic shot opportunities, and really exciting shooting. I had to restrict my shots to avoid dropping ducks on the far bank, which was a head-high wilderness of nettles, bramble and rush. The easiest ducks to retrieve were those that fell in the middle of the river, and my Labrador would be busily employed retrieving these as soon as they fell. If left,

above:
On the estuary

opposite:
A great opportunity

they would either drift into the shadowed edges or float off downstream. The dog work was aggravated by the steeling palings at the water's edge, which were there to contain the river and prevent erosion. Even a Labrador struggled to scrabble over these, so it was necessary to unload and put down the gun before taking the retrieve and then hauling the dog on to dry land.

On one October evening we had three duck on or over the far bank and, rather than leave them for fox food, I stripped off and swam the river so as to work my dog, which had lost heart. One of these duck he soon found where it floated out of sight in a shadowed reedy little bay. The other two were in the bankside cover and, being without any clothes, I was severely stung while encouraging my dog to hunt for these. I was eventually rewarded by two more successful retrieves and made the short swim back with three fat mallard ducks.

The main species of duck that visited my fen shoot was mallard. At a numerical peak in September, their numbers would decrease during the winter months but there was at all times a resident population of them. In the early days there was also a flock of tufted duck that lived on the river. Having shot and eaten one of these small diving duck, I made it a rule that any gun shooting a tufted would have to eat it. Several guns shot one but none, to my knowledge, shot a second. For those unfamiliar with the taste of tufted duck, I would describe it as being akin to a stale bread roll impregnated with methane. I once tried the trick of first boiling a tufted duck to extract the fat from the carcass. This caused a foul grey scum to form on the top of the boiling water and rendered the flesh inedible, while in my opinion doing nothing whatsoever to improve the foetid taste.

In contrast, such wigeon as occasionally visited were most welcome, both for the sport they provided and for the table. If we could shoot sufficient we would always have our wigeon cold smoked. For some reason, probably related to the fat content, smoked wigeon are delicious; a true gourmet's treat. However, although my shoot was less than 10 miles distant from the Welney Washes, which are famous for their huge over-wintering wigeon population, such incursions were irregular and infrequent.

Teal were to be found on the dykes and I developed a useful technique for stalking these. With all my dykes being straight, and often flailed so that the steep banksides were bare, great caution was required. I would approach the dyke in a low crouch, often crawling the last few yards. Then I would take a good long look, sometimes using binoculars to scan hard to see locations towards the ends of the dyke. Often there would be no duck at home, but sometimes this careful,

prolonged glassing would reveal the tell-tale shape of teal in the margins. Then it was game on! I would try to mark the little duck, which was difficult on the often featureless dyke bank. Then I would retreat and walk in a semi-circle out of sight before again approaching the dyke at what I adjudged to be the correct location. If I got this right, short-range shots at the springing teal would give me my best chance. More likely, the teal would have moved in the meantime or my marking would be out, making the resultant shot, if any, a difficult one.

One of our main drains was in a different league to the narrow field drains. About 20 yards wide and 15 feet below the level of the adjoining fields, it could hold a lot of duck, mainly mallard but sometimes wigeon, goldeneye and teal. When we had guest guns with us for a foray at our fen pheasants, we would pad out the day with a team stalk. This involved us locating the position of some duck on this drain and lining out the guns in such a way that they advance in line abreast across the adjacent field, no shooting being allowed until the drain was reached and the duck sprung. Some guns, particularly those whose shooting was restricted to maize game – reared pheasants and partridges from game covers – greatly enjoyed the tension and anticipation of this stalk. Jumping a duck from a fen drain may, in the grand scheme of things, hardly be

the highest form of sport, but time and again I have seen a good game shot fire two unavailing barrels at the departing duck and stand there mystified as to the reason for missing what were apparently the easiest of quarry shots.

This manoeuvre often concluded with some testing dog work. Such duck as fell on the drain were usually readily retrieved by the dogs. The second barrel kills would usually fall out on the field beyond the far bank. This necessitated the gundogs descending our bank, swimming the dyke, scrabbling up the near sheer bank on the other side, and then working well out in the far side field. The best dog for this was invariably a rangy, long-legged Labrador, and the worst would be close working, short-legged cockers and springers. However, my son had a highly intelligent sprocker who, even when passed her best years, would make the trip and proudly swim back with a mallard drake or duck.

Many years ago three of us accounted for 27 mallard while flighting a stubble field. On another very rough evening on the river bank I picked 13 mallard to my own gun. Those were exceptional flights and, more often than not, the time and effort invested in the evening's sport would be rewarded by just a couple of duck. However, there were and are many hidden benefits of seeing the day out in the fens. The wide, empty sky makes twilight time especially attractive. The steely wave

opposite:
In the bag!

on the water awakens the hunter's hopes. The warblers in the reeds, the call of the moorhen and the barn owl hunting the river bank are all part of that distinctive panorama where the original landscape was long ago remodelled by man.

There are of course places where there are really large numbers of wildfowl. Only last season, I was lucky enough to flight a pond in Cumbria's Eden valley. The estate keeper told me he had saved a pond for me and my team – we were four in all – and after a day's rough shooting we dropped into our butts, which were positioned below the earth dam of a decent-sized hill pond. The keeper had told me this was one of 20 ponds on the estate. As usual, while we waited for the flight to start, there was little activity and we were able to relax after an energetic day's walked up shooting mainly in the white grass on the edge of the moor – unusual terrain for guns from the south.

Suddenly, without any preliminary circling, three mallard dropped in before any of us could shoot. That was our wake-up call and we were ready for the next party. For some minutes the mallard flighted and then as they stopped coming, the teal started. I had never seen anything like it; the teal came in packs of 20 or 30 strong, slipping in over our shoulders from the valley behind and below us and turning into the wind to alight on the pond. At our shots, they would flare and split in all directions and in seconds be lost in the gloaming. Last of all we heard the wonderful whistle of wigeon returning to the pond, and some of these were added to the bag. It truly was a flight to remember!

As that was a memorable flight for wild duck, so our mornings on Milton Loch are imprinted on my mind for wild geese. It's with great happiness and gratitude I recall exchanging good morning greetings with Richard Pickup, our congenial and enthusiastic host at Craigadam, Crocketford, Dumfriesshire. When the party was assembled, Richard took us to the hills above the loch and dropped us off into natural hides behind stone walls and in forestry margins, where we waited on the coming daylight. In the lessening darkness, the steel sheen of the loch below us could be seen more and more clearly. Sometimes objects with the shape of geese could be seen. We waited, each of us alone in our hides, with anticipation conflicting with cold, in the hope that the chill wind would keep the geese down to a shootable height.

And then, if we were lucky, the geese would arrive overhead, arriving as deer do: without warning. And in that moment of engagement, the greylag appears to have nothing in common with his feral cousin. In his skein, he nurdles and side slips the stiff wind and flies wild. Even now, years later, I have my personal cameo of the big gander I had selected falling with an audible thwack just a few yards behind me and then, a few minutes later, a second, smaller goose dropping to a shot on the grass pasture.

Much closer to home, on a marsh-ringed estuary, lives my Rabelasian friend, King Henry. A man well beloved, he lives life to the full and as if each day may be his last. He has, with great generosity, taken me out both on his grass marshes and on the foreshore that he owns and controls. In the low places and scrapes on the short grass pasture, splashes form, and here he has placed me to try for a goldie or a wigeon easing in from the estuary, usually too late for my eyes to see or for me to shoot. When the weather is dry the grass pasture does not attract duck and he has put me out on the salt marsh, where in the dying light I have stood in a gutter with the distinctive, fascinating esturine life being carried on around me. Flights of waders fly over the estuary water, the water itself flows dark and slightly sinister, and the failing day changes by the minute. All the time I watched and waited and, after missed chances due to not seeing the duck, shot a singleton drake teal silhouetted against the sky. A solitary figure in a darkening seascape, my happiness was complete.

Woodcock! Woodcock!

We had followed the Warrener on a zigzag drive into north Devon, and none of us knew where we were when we pulled up at the gate to the forestry block. It looked like any other Forestry Commission wood to us, but back at the farmhouse, the previous evening, the Warrener had been optimistic. "Been left quiet for weeks," he said, in his broad Devon accent, "and your woodcocks like a discreet place."

He made them sound like a couple of lovers looking for a quiet place to park their car. We sipped our drinks and thought on that. In the mind's eye we could envisage the recently arrived woodcock resting under the larches. "It was full of woodcock when those Italians were here," he had added. He stressed the 'I' of Italian. We had heard from him that the Italians were lethal shots, but we didn't know whether that was to the detriment of the shooting party or the stocks of woodcock. One or two of us thought that if it was the woodcock, there wouldn't be so many left for us. Perish the thought, but the Italians could have shot the lot.

At least the Warrener was still on good form the next morning as he unloaded a rowdy pack of dogs, which one could just describe as spaniels or spaniel types, if you were being generous. "Come in Briar," called the Warrener, and a weasel dog slunk back to his heel. "Here, Blossom" - this in a more kindly tone as a liver and white bitch,

above:
Woodcock!
Woodcock!

definitely of springer origin, looked up at him adoringly.

"How's thou then, Echo?" he enquired of a long-legged animal that looked like the offspring of a greyhound and a springer spaniel. "That's the top dog for woodcock and for foxes!" the Warrener said to us. "When you hear old Echo bay, you need to look sharp."

By now the Warrener was placing us guns in the clear fell, but it wasn't like orthodox placing. "Here you," the Warrener said to Goodfellow, "you go to that fallen tree and stand there." He pointed to a tree stump 100 yards away.

Then, pointing out a line of old fir trees 50 yards to our right, he told me to go and stand by them. The other two guns were placed out of sight. I heard him shout at one of the dogs in the back of the wood, and then silence. I couldn't see we would do much good with four guns covering 400 yards around the perimeter of the larches, without any obvious line for the woodcock to take.

Then, from far away in under the trees, I heard a dog give tongue once, and then again and again until there was the mellifluous sound of Echo having a hunt. I half mounted my gun so that the barrels were raised and the stock rested against my chest. Had I not been warned to look sharp when Echo was in full cry?

A woodcock appeared over the top of the larches, heading straight towards me. I waited on it to make sure of a kill and,

instead of coming on, it dropped like a stone and passed within five yards of me three feet above the bracken and was gone before I could recover from my surprise. I looked up again and again at the empty sky in front of me where that woodcock had been, beating myself up for a missed chance.

There was another, but it flew below head height round the front of the wood before turning back over the Warrener. That one got away unshot at as it was never safe to shoot. The Warrener emerged from the undergrowth and I told him what had happened. He wanted to know why I had not shot at the second bird. "Low and dangerous," I replied. The Warrener sighed: "Those Italians would have shot that!"

The forestry didn't seem to be stuffed with woodcock, and plainly our circumspection in engaging what birds there were caused us to reduce our chances, but by the time we finished in the block we had bagged a couple and also gleaned a couple of cock pheasants that looked as if they had strayed in from the adjacent shooting estate, until we chanced on a discreet feeder, which the Warrener took the opportunity of replenishing as we were there.

From the forestry, we went back to somewhere – we never did find out where – in mid-Devon where there was a farm with steeply wooded banks beside a winding river. "This place always smells of woodcock," the Warrener said as we tumbled out of the truck, as keen as mustard for the next manoeuvre. We lined out on a sunken track between high Devon banks, with the gun at the top 250 feet above the gun at the bottom. Soon Echo was in good voice again, and a woodcock tried to make it across the river. The bottom gun nailed it and it fell on the far bank. Then, I had one I snatched at as it crossed the track, a lucky snap shot. Goodfellow at the top had nothing at all.

We had a bag of 10 head by lunch time and didn't stop for long. Over lunch the Warrener said he knew of a bank that was really warm and would be heaving with woodcock after the bitterly cold north-easterly winds we had been having. We walked the bank with our own dogs while Echo was given a well-earned rest. There were woodcock there all right, and the exercise yielded three fat birds, all in peak condition.

Off again, with the light fast fading by now, and we pulled up in yet another farm yard and struck off over the red Devon clay to head a small wood on a steep slope. I was the left-hand gun when a hen pheasant soared over me. I collected that one but missed the cock that followed her. Then I heard the unmistakable sound of Echo in full cry, and a woodcock was on the wing rising like a partridge over me. No mistake with that one, and a great way to end the day.

What a day! What a dog! Nearly 20 head shot over Echo, making a score of recollections that will endure into old age.

Another January trip after woodcock in the South West had been the woodcock hunter's equivalent of a wild goose chase. The soft, wet weather in Devon and Cornwall had gone through our choice coats, and the spares, and then through every other pac-a-mac and poncho we had in the truck for emergencies. In a few words, we got very wet. That didn't matter at all, but it hurt to find that after the anticipation, expectation, long journey, hard hunting days, and all that weather, the woodcock were just not there.

Our conversation was like that of a salmon fishing trip... replete with reasons for our failure. The woodcock had missed our ground as the nights of the last full moon had been foggy. It was too mild. And of course it was much, much too wet. The Russians had shot them all. It hadn't snowed sufficiently in Scandinavia. Some Jocks had shot a hatful each in south west Scotland or in the Hebrides. There was too much woodcock shooting; the stocks had been shot, but if we returned after the next full moon, next week, or maybe the week after that, then the woodcock would be in.

Taking my turn at the wheel, I drove north through the night and the dire phrase "woodcock in... woodcock in... woodcock in..." kept repeating itself in the recesses of my mind with the regularity of the revolutions of the wheels on the road.

Well, the woodcock hadn't been in and the efforts of my companions, dozing in the passenger seats of the truck, and my drying dogs, had all been fruitless. We weren't whingers and had endured some thin days in the past; had taken what came, paid our bills and moved on to the next shoot. We were no complainers, but none of us had ever previously shot three days straight in the West Country version of a cold shower. "Unrelenting rain," said Andrew in a plummy voice as he woke up in the front passenger seat. "Never fired a cartridge!" mused Barry from the back.

"I'm shooting with the Colonel tomorrow," I said. The three of us were old friends and either couldn't hear or take any notice of what each other said, depending on the ambient noise level, our own morale, and other factors. Morale was certainly low tonight, and my brightest moment came when I thought of the dry jacket and breeks waiting for me in the cupboard at home.

Next morning, re-equipped, I was on my way to the Colonel's. I was not exactly dressed according to regulations. The only spare breeks I could find were a bargain mustard-coloured pair I had purchased imprudently at a game fair a decade before. My only serviceable dry shooting coat was in a creative camouflage pattern, and my stalking boots needed a clean. Never mind what the Colonel thinks, I thought to myself, I am not standing about and shooting another day in damp or wet clothes.

Arriving in the Colonel's yard, I only had a moment to enjoy the pleasing cameo of his pretty girl grooms in their tight jodhpurs before the Colonel was dressing me down on account of my fancy dress. No invitation into the kitchen for coffee for me that morning! Instead, an orders group in the yard, which all the guns found it hard to concentrate on as the grooms were now energetically mucking out the hunters. We were going to shoot the big wood. Well, we all knew that: the big wood was the shoot. Actually, it was half the big wood. In the old Colonel's day, the shoot comprised the whole of the big wood but, in revenge for years of being bossed about, the anarchic old pig farmer who owned the other half had willed it to some bug hunters. That's why, strictly speaking if you understand me, there was only half the wood left to shoot now in this the young Colonel's time.

As the young Colonel continued his briefing, I must admit my mind was meandering again, and I was not alone. By now, the blonde groom had quite unnecessarily taken off her heavy jacket and was pitching in with the fork and the broom in a way that emphasised her sizzling, sexy shape. At length we moved off, and it was not before time as Stud, an old regimental mucker of the young Colonel's, was showing signs of reluctance to come shooting at all and was heard muttering about the work being terribly heavy for these wee girls. However, the Colonel was having none of it, and dispatched Stud on a walking in exercise that took him to the other side of the farm.

The plan was to make good a few hedges and fields and push what birds there were in these into the big wood, and then have four drives in the big wood and another in an entirely separate cover some distance away. During the walking in exercise several pheasants either flew or ran into the big wood, but the partridges, refugees from the adjacent commercial shoot, mainly slipped out the side. A few had, however, been sheltering in an old pit and a brace of these went into the bag to open the day's account.

Once in the wood, my dogs and I were allocated a beating role in which we, with three other guns, were to dog out a neck of woodland to the standing guns. Any pheasants that went forward and escaped the guns would, the Colonel hoped, be encountered again later in the day. My spaniels set to with a will. They gave me the impression they were thinking that at least master had taken them somewhere dry. Several pheasants were flushed out of the brambles and, at the end of the drive, the Colonel declared himself well pleased with the half dozen that we had bagged.

Next, we were ordered to surround a compartment of Christmas trees and, as this was too thick to penetrate, the spaniels were allowed and encouraged to have free rein, assisted by a motley pack of hunt terriers which were enjoying – well, a terrier's holiday. The mayhem in the undergrowth caused quite a flurry of pheasants to flush, and I accounted for no less than three. As I

picked up, I reflected I had just equalled my total head count from my visit to Devon and Cornwall.

Next, there was what the Colonel called a NAFFI break, and there was no doubt of the success of this when the snacks and drinks, as we call them in Suffolk, were brought to the RV by the two grooms. In the old Colonel's day the drinks invariably consisted of tumblers of rum and ginger wine, and there had definitely not been any girl grooms, so I thought that went to show the old days were not always better than the present. In fact, standing there in the winter sunshine with a glass of something a little less lethal, I thought today was both drier by far and better than the previous one.

The next drive was the big one, a block of coppice woodland with plenty of good habitat and the Colonel's feeders as evidence that this was where the birds would be. Better still, I was allocated a spot that meant I was the right-hand front standing gun. The next gun to my left was on the main ride, but I was also able to look up and shoot above a lesser flank ride. I knew from long experience that this was likely to be a hot spot. "Hell Fire Corner for you, Barnes!" directed the Colonel, leaving me to make ready for the game.

Very soon I heard the shout of "Woodcock! Woodcock!" and saw the little brown bird was likely to cross the narrow ride in front of me. Swinging like mad, I dropped it and, reloading quickly, had another one over my left shoulder behind the line. The beating line was in full action now and there were cries of "Cock forward! Hen back! Woodcock!"

"Slow down! Slow down!" roared the Colonel, and some semblance of order was restored. On Hell Fire Corner I was whirling like a dervish, shooting at pheasants and woodcock making for the corner flag. It was great sport, and by the time the whistle went, I had four woodcock and three pheasants and should have had more.

I spent the rest of the day working the spaniels. I had had my great 'peg' at Hell Fire Corner, and it was the turn of the other guns.

A lot more rain has fallen on Devon and Cornwall since that memorable day when,

in Suffolk of all places, I shot twice as many woodcock as four of us had managed to bag in prime woodcock country down in the South West.

"Duncroke," repeated Greengrass doubtfully, when I explained we had a spare day, and wanted to shoot there. "The walking on Duncroke is mighty hard!"

But we were not to be denied, and in the half-light of a late December morning, we gathered at the old logging yard and made ready for what we thought would be a really rough day's shooting.

The frost was in the ground and it was far too cold to stand around, so we started with a pincer movement over some clear fell. In the half-light every step was attended by a

potential hazard. The spruce forestry had been cut years ago and replanted. There were holes and traps, roots and brash, and a drainage ditch every few yards. Great care was needed to stay standing, and the first pheasant to rise went away unshot at as the only gun that could have engaged it was unloaded in the bottom of a drainage channel. The only other one – a hen bird – was accounted for when it was flushed close to a feed hopper.

The next part of our plan involved sending three guns forward to the far end of a compartment of larches that looked manageable. Another gun and myself waited for them to drive round and get into position before we put the spaniels into the wood. Unseen by us under the branches, I suspect they ran riot, but I heard more than saw a woodcock flush and go forward and gave a good shout to forewarn the forward standing guns. After a long pause I heard a shot, and then two more shots. That could

mean anything, and I continued, struggling through the terrible ground on the edge of the larches and, now and then, where there were gaps, going in to add my presence to that of the busy spaniels. We finished that impromptu 'drive' with two woodcock (it took three shots but they got the first one) and a pheasant.

The next section of replanted ground we went into was a nightmare. The cover was heavier than it had been in the first place, and hid the holes left by the forestry machinery. We floundered about in there for a while before giving up on it. Nearly an hour had been wasted, and the dogs had worked hard to no effect.

We decided to try the sides of the stream that ran through the bottom of the valley. The going was easier here, and we started with a snipe that flushed by an ancient stock fence. Then, working our way upstream, we picked up another couple of woodcock before eventually climbing on to the forestry road. Time for a break and a piece off the bonnet of the truck. The sun had come out and, although it promised to turn cold again later, the day was a perfect one on which to be out with a dog and a gun.

In the afternoon, we moved the vehicles to the other end of the ground and decided to try what had been a belt of trees long before the estate had been planted for forestry. In places there were the remains of iron railings and gates and, with a stretch of the imagination, it was just possible to imagine how fine – and how different – the place must have looked 100 years previously when it was the seat of some successful Scottish son of the industrial revolution. More prosaically, it was a derelict belt of trees with much fallen and grown over stuff. As I staggered through the wrecked landscape, lurching from foothold to foothold in the uneven ground, I tried to keep alert for the woodcock that would be pushed out by the dogs, and was rewarded with one that went away fast and low over the young trees. This bird took some time for the dogs to find even though I had it marked down to a specific, distinctive stump.

When we came to the end of the belt there was nothing for it but to make our way out to the road through what was near thicket. In the course of this we flushed and shot a cock pheasant. As we neared the other end I noticed my spaniel slowing down and kept a careful eye on him. It was just as well I did, for after a few more yards, he went down and I had to pick him up and carry him in my arms out to the road, mercifully only a few yards in front, where I fed him a few slices of Mars Bar to reinstate his sugar levels. Towelled dry, put in his bag, I knew from past experience he would soon recover from the day.

The light was going fast now and that left us just the flight. After a break and a cup of tea, it was time to line out between two blocks of trees and, blissfully, the only walking required was a stroll on the road.

The sun had gone and the temperature was dropping sharply; it was already back below freezing. Even with an extra fleece it was really cold, but not so cold that I couldn't look back with pleasure and amusement on the rigorous, challenging day we had just enjoyed. Any day that has springer spaniels off their feet by the finish of it has to have been a good one. We had only a very modest bag, but had had huge fun achieving it.

Then, as the last of the light was squeezed out of the sky, the first woodcock topped the trees in front and, for just a few minutes, it seemed there were woodcock everywhere. These were not the full-sized lumbering woodcock of full daylight, but shadows of 'cock, fast flighting and snipe-sized in the gloaming. Shots were made successfully, shots taken and missed and then, as suddenly as it had started, the flight finished. The pick up was a nightmare in the dark with such tired dogs as we still had on their feet – my old chap was out of it – but after 20 minutes or so we picked the last of the five we had down.

We were a way down the main road south – heading home that same night – when my companion stirred in the passenger seat. "Hard walking at Duncroke," he said, "and I am done and only fit to croak!" And with that he went straight back to sleep, leaving me to my recollections of the fast-flying shadows of woodcock at flight.

A downside of the stag stalking season was that the spaniels were not welcomed

above:
Setting out for the
day's sport

or required so, for them, there was a lot of lazing around while the master was out on the hill at the stags. Years ago I would have given them a serious day at the grouse but, with the scarcity of these, I took them out for snipe instead. Parking the truck on the south side of McKay's Croft gave me a choice of start points. As the spaniels were full of beans, I headed out to the west where a burn wended its slow way through a snipe-likely marshy bit of ground.

Typically, I bumped a fat snipe within 25 yards of starting and, I am ashamed to say, before I had loaded my gun. I was, in my disappointment, quite unable to explain why a snipe should choose that place over the many other more obviously favourable acres available to it. That said, I should have been ready.

Arriving at the burn, I decided to work the wet ground on my side of it and then to take the other bank upstream after I had found a crossing point. The near side proved to be blank, although the spaniels wholly roared into it and hunted out the wet grass and reeds with huge enthusiasm. I had to go downstream a distance until the burn ran shallower over some stones and crossed it there with the dogs before turning upstream again. There was more wet ground this side, and I was ready for the snipe that flushed with that distinctive rasp their wings make as they get airborne. I didn't give this one any quarter and fairly floored it before it had gone 20 yards.

The experts say you must shoot snipe early before they start to jink, or late after they have finished. What luck I have had with them has usually derived from shooting as quickly as I can. "Shoot fast!" is my mantra while snipe shooting, and as I continued through the wet ground I repeated it to myself several times, but no more snipe obliged. Then, having to get some height to cross over the burn without getting wet feet, I went up a knoll that had some nice heather on it and, noting the interest suddenly being shown by the dogs, flushed a covey of grouse. I killed the first bird cleanly as it was going right handed but snatched my second barrel at another going directly away. The spaniels were on the first one in a flash and the old dog brought it back with his tail wagging. I am sure my dogs find the scent of grouse the most strongly smelling and addictive of all game birds.

After this bonus, I crossed the road and headed over the ridge towards the head of Loch Murrone. I knew there was a curious area here, a couple of acres in extent, comprising quaking wet peat in which the summer's green water weeds were beginning by now to die back. I couldn't go on this stuff but it took the dogs' weight without any problem, and they were both keen enough to hunt the place while I supervised from the shore. Where it was at its widest a small wisp of snipe flushed, and although I tried a shot at the nearest bird, they were really too far as they flew away across the loch. On the far side there was another boggy place that looked promising, and a small snipe jumped from the edge of

a curious rocky island in the middle of this and, just before I was going to fire at it, I recognised it as a jack snipe, and let it go on its way.

I then had a bit of a walk to the best bog on the estate, which was of a triangular shape and provided plenty of scope for the spaniels having, in places, plenty of cover. One snipe, which had taken advantage of this to sit tight, went away behind me at an angle and, by the time I had got onto it, there was no question of taking it early. It looked as if it was a mile away. I swung as far in front as I could and fired and, to my amazement, saw it glide down. I walked over, never taking my eyes off the place it had landed, and had the dogs hunt there. Even though my marking was perfect, the small bird had moved a yard or two and several minutes elapsed in hunting for it and bringing it to hand. I was disappointed not to flush another snipe or two from that good spot, but walked over the watershed to where I knew of another good place, and shot one more there before taking a route over the top of some knolls back to my truck. Three snipe and a grouse was a good bag for an afternoon foray, and with the snipe for starters and the grouse (luckily a young one) for a main course, there were also the makings of a decent supper.

I was on my own that afternoon and, while walking back at the finish of it, I thought of the satisfaction I had had in snipe shooting, often quite unexpectedly. One ordinary October day I had visited my

fen shoot – Lark Hall Farm – to deal with some chores, and had come across snipe in numbers in a field of potatoes. That crop was deeply ridged and baulked up, with flooded trenches between the ridges after local heavy rain that afternoon. There were no more than two or three inches of standing water, but that must have been enough to bring the worms up and into reach of the snipe. With the potato crop still in full green leaf, the snipe held while I hunted them and I had good sport there that afternoon.

On another occasion, an innocuous field of rape was heaving with snipe which, when driven downwind, flew high and wide and escaped unscathed. Those were wild driven snipe and, in that mode, completely different from one seeking to escape from under a bank or out of a gateway in frosty weather, when running water or cattle or whatever have kept a small place open for it to feed.

I reflected on the many miles I had walked over the years, and the intense satisfaction I had derived from trying to shoot woodcock and snipe. Although my bags were always small, my pleasure was great. I remembered Lord Home's dictum on the three essential ingredients for fieldsports: a distinctive landscape, good exercise, and a worthwhile quarry. I felt that more often than not all these had been achieved, and never more so than when I shot woodcock on 'the Island', which I have done many times.

There is a long tradition of travelling to the Scottish islands for sporting shooting. However, I had little time for tradition that morning as 'the General' and I were to shoot the island's north shore, and no sooner was I awake than in my mind's eye I was already seeing the braes and burns we would hunt with our spaniels.

My springer spaniel, Brandy, had suspect stamina in the cold and wet so I fed him a warm milk and porridge breakfast, the remnants of which the little cocker, Lark, scoffed with gusto. For sure, the work of these two foot soldiers would underpin the success of our sport that day. A short drive to our starting point took us round the north coast with the sea just a stone's throw from the track and several diminutive Hebrides islands in the distance. There would be time enough to admire the view after we had made some height. For now, we negotiated the stock fence and headed up the hill.

Almost at once we were climbing through a mature hardwood with magnificent mature beech, oak and other trees. I soon came to a burn, the banks of which became increasingly steep as we ascended.

The two spaniels meanwhile were raring to hunt, but I kept Brandy at heel for the time being. The wood floor was mainly bare of cover and there was no need for him to waste his energy there.

20 minutes later I emerged out of the woodland at the second stock fence, beyond which was the prospect of the open hill. I waited until the General showed on my left and waved his intention of following an old dyke studded with stunted bushes and patches of bracken. My own frontage featured the upper reaches of the stream I have already mentioned, which now had a nice bank for hunting on its east side and a grassy flat to the west. I elected to walk this side and set Brandy to hunt the bank.

If ever there was one, this was a place that spoke of woodcock; here in the discreet braes above the burn were numberless places for woodcock to rest. Out on the illimitable hill, where the wild black cattle roam, there was

feeding a-plenty. I carried my gun ready for instant action, and I was already mounting it as the woodcock rose and flew low and directly away from me. A snap shot and it was down in a clump of reeds. I sent Brandy at once and in seconds he was at the fall, with my expectation reaching fever pitch as he feathered to the scent and brought the mottled brown bird to hand in fine style.

I took a minute or two to admire this beautiful bird – my quarry – and smooth the ruffled feathers before stowing it carefully in my old game bag. Then, with a wave to the General, who was by now flanking way out on the higher ground on some foray of his own, I pushed on up the burn.

Quite soon Brandy owned to another scent and returned several times to the bole of a stunted tree, but no bird rose. I heard a double report from my son's gun and then felt I was through the prime ground, being now too far out on the hill and too high for woodcock. Although I persisted for another 200 yards, there was no flush and, leaving the burn, I worked round the shoulder of the hill towards a patch of whins that looked more promising. The General had spotted this too, and signalled that he would take a line downhill of the bushes.

I entered Brandy, who went in with relish and soon flushed a pair of 'cock. One slipped out unsaluted, but the other sprung high like a teal and fell to a stylish shot from the General's gun. That's one each and a brace of woodcock by 11 o'clock.

above:
The mystic bird

Taking an impromptu break, we enjoyed the distinctive Hebrides sea view from 750 feet, and I pointed out Mora Island where, it is said, two guns once accounted for over 100 woodcock in a day. Enough said! For us, 10 would be a dream day.

Setting off again, we planned a rough route that would take us downhill through what looked like a snipe bog, and then into some interesting scrub woodland which we could see on the rising ground the other side. The bog produced a single snipe which fell to my gun. As so often with snipe, there were agonising moments of uncertainty before Brandy brought the morsel to me almost hidden in his mouth. That bird then joined the woodcock in my bag.

In spite of the success with the snipe, I was not sorry when I had completed the crossing of the bog as the walking was treacherous, and the higher ground was altogether easier. Here there was much bracken, brown and half down now after the attentions of the winter frost and snow. This cover enabled Brandy and Lark to demonstrate their best work and they turned out three or four 'cock, two of which went into the game bag,

but in more than two shots. With two couple of 'cock and the snipe we stopped for our piece, with the General carefully selecting a sheltered spot on the hillside that gave a spectacular sea view. We each ate with the spaniels flopped at our feet, waiting ready to scrounge for crusts. We had had a first-rate morning and were well pleased with both our dogs and our shooting. And with an afternoon still to go and a flight this evening, there was sure to be more sport ahead.

As it happened, the afternoon disappointed. We tackled the expanses on the lower west end of the hill and found the cover on it to be too widespread for just the two of us. We tried cherry picking the most likely looking spots, but without any luck. Then the dogs, visibly tiring now, put up two woodcock in quick succession, when they were ranging out further than they should have been. Our combined efforts resulted in one more 'cock, and I had not added to my two and the snipe. As we came off the hill, we looked forward to a cup of tea before the flight.

This foray entailed us climbing up the slopes yet again from sea level, and then taking up station on open, rough grassland outside a forest block.

I chose the lower position and, as the light faded, noted that while I could see well enough on the downhill side, a woodcock uphill of my stand would soon be lost against the hillside background. Meanwhile Brandy (shivering from a mixture of cold, fatigue and excitement) and I awaited the coming of the woodcock. If they were to flight that night then they would flit out at last light. There, high on the hill, the night slowly strangled the dying day and it was good to wait, eyes straining to see the first woodcock. Time stood still on the timeless hillside, and no birds were seen.

Then, like a ghost bird, a woodcock passed close by my left-hand (uphill) side and I snapped a shot at it into the murk behind, and had no idea whether I had hit or missed. A minute later another flighted high, wide, and silently to my right. I stretched out over the void with a deliberate lead and shot it. Stricken, it set its wings and glided down into the rushes 100 yards below me. That would be the devil to pick! A lull followed and then one more, a crosser this time, which I killed cleanly in front, and then (as suddenly as it had begun) the flight was over and the pick up began.

Brandy picked the crosser quickly and then, at my bidding, hunted above and behind me for the first bird. It was dark by this point and I slipped on a head lamp and encouraged Brandy until, to my delight, he returned with my woodcock.

This left just the downhill bird and my son joined me – having completed his own pick up – with Lark for this final search. Brandy was all in by now but the younger bitch was still game for a hunt and, after working the reeds, pulled uphill several yards and made a clever retrieve. I silently blessed her.

Back by the seashore, we turned out our game bags and counted the total for the day: 11 woodcock and the snipe. Five woodcock and one snipe are mine so Brandy and I had shot our share. More important, the General and I were now two tired, happy men, with exhausted dogs, who had all enjoyed an exceptional day in superlative surroundings.

Later, with the dogs long since fed and abed, we reviewed the incidents of the day's sport over fireside drinks. We could recall each woodcock flushed, and sketched for each other cameos of our spaniels quartering the bracken and the whin. We heard again that thrilling rasp made by the 'cocks wings as they flushed and rose from cover. We dwelt awhile longer on our flight time, when the winter-pale colours had seeped out of the hill face, and we had taken our last light chances with a mystic bird in a wild place.

Time enough for tradition now, and we remembered the earlier days we had spent enjoying Scottish sporting shooting, and the good dogs with whom we had shared our triumphs and disappointments. This most memorable day of ours was, we thought, one within the tradition of true shooting men and glorious spaniels. And during our day we had enjoyed a secret island, entire unto ourselves; a winter place so beautiful that even torture would not compel us to say its name. Sleepily now, we raised benign glasses to old shooting men and to the spaniel in his role as the rough shooter's friend.

Red Letter Days

The late Lord Forte – the hugely successful hotelier – once hosted a day on his shoot in and about Ickworth Park in Suffolk, in the course of which a bag in excess of 900 pheasants was accumulated. In response to my natural enquiry of his former gamekeeper as to whether his Lordship had been pleased with that, I was told that he had not been at all happy by reason of their failure to shoot 1,000 pheasants that day. He was, the keeper added, a man who was never satisfied with the size of the day's bag. Plainly, the large numbers of birds shot that day failed to make it a red letter day for him, as he had wanted more.

In my opinion, although I enjoy 'getting stuck in' as much as the next man, the numbers of birds shot does not in itself make for an exceptional day for me. I remember being invited to shoot a day at a well-known commercial shoot, and arriving on a snowy morning to find the bag shot the previous day lying on the lawn under a light covering of snow. The gun bus was filthy and had obviously not been cleaned since the start of the season, if then. There were plenty of birds, both pheasants and partridges, and they flew well so there were no complaints on that score. However, all day long, the picking up team was loud and in our faces, and the last straw was when the head picker up drove up in his white pick-up truck and parked it 50 yards behind me on a knoll of higher ground. The lunch was doubtless nutritious, but lacking in any discernible taste, and the wine originated in some creek or other.

That was never going to be a red letter day. The hardened operator could quite easily have injected and sustained some charm and grace into the day. The previous day's bag in the game larder, the gun bus spruced up, the pickers up brought to heel, the food and wine improved, and it would have been in with a chance. However, what we were experiencing was game shooting reduced to an industrial process and, unless the guns were chosen from those solely devoted to killing birds, then the point of a good day's shooting had been almost entirely missed.

On the subject of the quality of the birds, a failure by the management to make any effort to show birds well disqualifies that shoot from being considered for a red letter tag. The birds should be presented so as to provide the guns with the most testing opportunities. With this in mind, my young friend and fellow shooting enthusiast, Sam, takes his gun teams to his famous Blinder Drive after lunch when, on a winter's day, the sun is bright and low over the hill from which the game flies in profusion. The gun without a good pair of sunglasses is in a lot of trouble here, and so are many of those who actually remembered their shades.

Blinder is such a difficult drive to shoot

above:
Partridges by
the Halladale

that the kill-to-cartridge ratio rarely looks impressive. I only hope all the guns that shoot it are candid enough to acknowledge how many more pheasants and partridges they could have added to the bag had their shooting skills been more accomplished. In my estimation, a shoot manager or keeper who puts such thought into his drives is always going to stand more chance of putting on red letter days than those lacking that enthusiasm and energy.

For a couple of seasons I had a gun in a historic shoot that had a lot going about it for a shooting man. The 'Big House' was historic and the lunch room as impressive as the lunch served, with all the ingredients being bred or grown on the estate. The regular guns, gamekeepers and supporting staff were all cheerful chaps and, joy of joys, the shooting was almost all over light land. Partridges flew well early in the season, and later some good pheasants were shown. All these positive points were outweighed by the invariable tactic of the estate to fill the expected bag before lunch. The keeper would slip in a heavy 'meat' drive when it was least expected, and the guns would then retire to lunch knowing they would be turned out for the afternoon on one of the tenanted pig farms with very low expectations of any sport at all. In my book, a day's shooting is a day's shooting and I became disillusioned with such afternoon drives, which were almost pointless because of the lack of game.

Worse still, the pig farms were adjacent to a busy main road and so were accompanied by the roar of passing traffic. When I realised that even I, for all my enthusiasm, wasn't enjoying that routine at all, I dropped out of the syndicate and found some better sport elsewhere. In my next selection, I paid more attention to the whereabouts of the shoot. It's not impossible to shoot next to main roads and rail lines, but it is hardly relaxing, particularly when the gun has a dog with him and has to worry about him being run over. For this reason, I would say that a shoot needs to be in attractive countryside and relatively free from transport noise pollution to be in with a chance of hosting red letter days.

Another factor likely to make for a great day is that the other guns are all personal guests of the host and that no money has changed hands. The guests are then aware of the huge privilege and kindness of their generous host and he has the pleasure and satisfaction of putting on the day he wants for them and making it go well. There is, in my experience, often a difference in attitude between guns who have paid for their day's shooting and those who are being treated. The fact that the next day or next week the guest may be treating the host is neither here or there to this subtle pleasure shared by guns on a private day on a private shoot.

The gun who is assessing the day, perhaps as he drives home afterwards, needs to have shot reasonably well. Good marksmanship is not generally that important but the gun who says of a day that it was a day to remember, will be more likely to do so if he can remember the glorious chances that he took.

In a list of requirements for the makings of a red letter day I have one more ingredient to add. The day must, for whatever reason, be a good shooting day for the shoot. Conditions – breeze strength and direction, temperature, barometer pressure, cloud cover and so on – should combine to make the game more testing on the wing than it would likely be on a still, dank day on that shoot. With these demanding criteria in mind, I realise that I am very fortunate to have so many wonderful days from which to choose my red letter days. I must start with a day in the early 1970s when I was shooting with the great merchant prince, Ronald Arthur Vestey.

We met that morning at Great Thurlow Hall at ten to nine in the morning, and RAV liked to be away by five to. That morning, in a team of eight, there were generals, brigadiers, and an admiral bristling with war-won medals, distinguished senior men in the autumn of their lives. And there was myself, the indulged son of the squire's parson.

That morning we were to shoot the biggest wood on the estate and, like all the

woods, it was perfectly maintained by the forestry manager and his team of foresters. Everything that could be done had been done to assist the game shooting and, as we got out of the Land Rover for the first drive, in the thin winter sunshine, I felt a great anticipation. I was drawn number seven and had one of RAV's kinsmen at six and a senior officer at eight. "I feel really ill," whispered the kinsman, "But I'm not going to give up my shooting today." I looked at him and the poor man was grey with pain.

The drive started and, being on a side ride, I was snap shooting. By my usual standards in those dire days when, as I have explained, I hit virtually nothing, I was on good form and I picked up seven pheasants at the end of the drive. The next drive was out of the Thicks and at peg number one I had a quiet drive by a tall hedge, claiming just the three down there. I was number three at Stubbins, a smaller wood from which the pheasants flew back to the big wood, which was called Trundley. Drinks then and, although I was keeping a low profile, that most gallant of soldiers, the late Major General Peter Gregson, made a point of talking fishing to me. Even late in life, he had an irrepressible zest for fieldsports and racing and a natural stylish charm. He talked me through a pool he had fished for salmon on the River Lochy, bringing to life the way the fly swung across the stream and

how a silver fresh 12-pound salmon had lunged at the fly and how he had landed it after a hard fight.

I was still shooting well – exceptionally well by my abysmal standards – when we went to the Grove on the other side of Trundley. It was full of pheasants and there was shooting all along the line with myself right in the thick of it. I had a hatful and so it went on, with all the guns realising by now we were on for a huge day.

At last we went to our pegs in the wide ride separating the Thorns from the rest of the wood. The Thorns was the day's last drive, and from the start pheasants flew forward well, giving challenging shots above the tall oaks and beeches. We shot and shot and, having used all the cartridges in my pockets, I had to refill from my bag.

At the sound of the horn, I unloaded and put down my gun with shaking hands. I had never shot such a drive or shot so well.

Back in RAV's purpose-built lunch room, his hospitable hand steered his guests through the lunch to coffee and a sweep on the day's bag. Then he announced the total: 655 head. My own contribution was, I thought, 63, so I had for once shot my share of the bag. Now that was a red letter day! It took place many years ago now and the gallant General and most other members of that team have moved on.

opposite:
'A fine flush'

As Hemingway once observed, they have done what every man has to do.

The eagerly-awaited day in early December came when I was to go as a guest to Rookery Farm. The morning was bitterly cold, several degrees below freezing, when I set off in the dark. Past experiences over, perish the thought, nearly 50 years, suggested to me that the covering of snow and hard frost would result in us having an exceptional day. Arriving in good time in the yard, I saw from the happy look on my host's face that this was going to be good. He told me that one gun had pulled the previous evening and, rather than replace him, we were to shoot seven guns. I recognised each of them as they trickled into the house for coffee; these were guns I had shot with here for years. Already there was some good craic, a pleasant mixture of shooting and farming talk, brought to order for a briefing. Like many hosts on his own shoot, he was pretty firm with the guns. I drew number one and, on the right-hand end of the line, opened my account with two cock pheasants. I looked down the line to the gun behind the oak tree in the hedge, where a school boy may perhaps have wiped the great, late, Albert Steele's eye.

Next to another cover, a cunning drive with the birds being flushed away from the guns and flagged back. I had several there and then a surprisingly quiet drive in the wood when we shot Fox Grove.

At the end of that drive my old springer spaniel cleaned up a couple of excellent retrieves.

Wandering companionably back through the wood for mid-morning drinks, I had no idea that the day – relatively quiet until now – was suddenly going to take off. As we waited to shoot Pig Field behind the farm, I was one from the end of the line when the partridges started to come. Behind me was the wet holding wood, that occupied the lower part of the slope that rose behind us on the other side of a small stream. We were standing on rising ground with a tall hedge in front of us and the partridges were getting up way back and rising to take first the hedge and then the wood. I shot like a man possessed! I was swinging like a dervish to lead them and they were falling one after another until I had seven for eight shots and half a dozen cracking good pheasants.

I don't record this triumph in a boastful way. Not at all! It was just a rare and precious golden moment in a long shooting career, and one that I shall never forget. The rest of the day was wonderful, but without my ever reaching the heights achieved in that fantastic drive.

That afternoon, as I said goodbye to the team of volunteers who make these Rookery Farm days so wonderful, one of them smiled and said, "Enjoyed yourself at Pig Field, didn't you David? That was pretty to watch."

I dare say I purred with pride, as that home team are not readily impressed. And that was definitely a red letter day!

"I want you to come to my new shoot," my friend, Ben, said one time.

"Have you joined another syndicate?" I replied. Ben is always up for more shooting. "Not really," he answered, "I've just taken a couple of guns for a day on the coast in early November."

I met Ben at the local pub for breakfast on the appointed day. I was excited by the prospect of a new shoot and new ground, somewhere Ben had told me that had the scent of the salt marshes about it. He had given me the impression the day would be a light one, with just a few pheasants and partridges, but I didn't know what to expect.

When we went into the pub, I was glad to find that though the shoot was to be a new one, the faces of the other guns were almost all old ones that I recognised very well. It's always good fun to shoot with guns you know through shooting, but that you don't shoot with all the time. In several cases, we had a lot of catching up to do. Over breakfast, the conversation became more general and it was obvious that whatever we shot we would have some fun during the day. Then, we all took a short drive to the RV and pulled on our boots for the shoot.

As it happened, I recognised the dropping off point for the first drive, as it was in the entrance to a flight pond I had once shot. We didn't go to that but took a track through some thick woodland, and then crossed a dyke and went out into a rough meadow. The host dropped off numbers one and two here as flank guns, and took the rest of us over another dyke that had tall alders on either side of it, over which any birds reaching numbers one and two would have to fly. As number three, my peg was in the angle made by the alders of this dyke and the wood line behind me. It looked a promising spot, and it was.

No sooner had the beaters started to blank in some game cover in front of me than I was engaged in my own little shoot. Pheasants and partridges were drawn to my corner and presented nicely. They made inviting shots I was keen to take on and, encouraged by the shoot captain standing at my shoulder, I did just that. I had a super stand and let sufficient game through to number two, whose peg I could easily have spoiled, for him to have an even better one. By the end of the drive, I was very grateful to the shoot captain as, being a new boy and a guest there, I would have been reluctant to shoot so freely without his support. As it was, he had made it absolutely clear I was to engage the game. A difficult pick up across the dykes and in the wet wood behind ensued, and suffice to say I needed help carrying my game back to the game cart. A great

start! Ben slapped my back and said he wouldn't bring me again if I shot so many.

In the next drive, my peg was adjacent to a number of pens, in which hen pheasants belonging to the owner's closed flock were pecking at the feeders – quite unconcerned by the disturbance caused by the drive. Here, I had a number of pheasants and partridges that skimmed through and I just had to pick out the best of these and leave the rest. The ones to my right were rising and giving the next gun better shooting than they would have given me so I was happy to leave them for him.

When we stopped for a drink one of the guns and I reminisced about a day's shooting we had shared in the Sussex and Hampshire Downs, and the fine birds we had shot or, in my case, shot at, there. We agreed that the shoot was as good as any we had shot on and that we had not had a bad drive there at all. I laughed at the memory, and told him I had watched one gun, presented with high and low birds, pick the lowest one out of the pack. There, I said, was a man who simply did not appreciate tall pheasants.

With preparations being made for the next drive, I was asked if I minded acting as a walking gun. "Not at all!" I replied and, as the beaters and I disembarked from the trailer to go to the back of the drive, I welcomed the chance as there was a stiffening breeze in our faces which surely meant some birds would come back on the wind. Dropping in behind the beaters, I was on the left-hand side of a wide strip of maize with a belt of trees on the other side of it, but out of shot. As the drive developed a lot of game went forward. The birds that took a route over the low numbered guns struggled into the wind, but those curling over five, six and seven were all challenging birds on that breeze. As for my chances, they were downright difficult, with the partridges in particular coming like rockets as they headed for the safety of the estuary flood bank. I had five down but in more than five shots, and needed help from the pickers up to pick them. When a gun is walking behind the beaters it's almost impossible for him to keep a mark on the fallen, and that's made even more difficult when the cover comprises head-high maize.

By now I was really enjoying the shooting on this 'new shoot', having already had some good drives and exciting shooting. The partridges in the last drive had been as good as you would see anywhere and made for difficult, exciting, testing shooting. To those people who despise East Anglia game, I would just say it was well worthwhile getting out of bed to shoot at these.

By this stage, I had seen much of the landscape of this shoot. We had started on the edge of a wet, dyke-surrounded wood with almost tropical growth in its under storey. We had stood in open fields and had drives from higher bits of ground; sandy outcrops for the most part. We had seen the wide, closely cropped grass pastures, the sheep grazing, separated from the estuary by the sea wall. With its wide open spaces and the silvered steel surface of the river there was something awesome about the landscape of this place.

This sea wall was to feature hugely in the last drive of the day, when I was drawn number two and positioned on the left-hand side of it, just inland of the wall which was above me, with number one out of sight standing on the saltings. The other guns were spread out on the sheep grazing, standing proud on the cropped turf. I fancied my peg. I thought the game would be drawn to the line of the sea wall and would follow it.

I did not have long to wait to find my surmise was correct. Partridges began to skim forward, picking up speed in the now strong, gusting wind, and then turned to follow the bank of the sea wall. I found myself dealing with them one after another as they took this line, and I shot with unaccustomed lethality. Some were crossing, still heading seawards at that point, and one or two flew over my left shoulder, but mostly I was taking these fast-flying birds over the bank so that they fell into the long grass on it or into the deep, overgrown dyke underneath and on my side of it. That was a fantastic

drive on which to end. After another difficult, prolonged pick up, we walked off the grass marsh in the low light of the winter afternoon leaving that place to the lapwing and the curlew, the plaintive calls of which evoked the comings and goings of the steeled tide race.

Back in the pub, there was a glass of wine and a good meal and the companionable chat of old shooting friends. We unwound, as they say, after the excitements and exertions of the shooting day. Come the time, I thanked the shoot owner, said goodbye to the other guns and took a breath of fresh air with my friend. We didn't say a lot: we didn't need to say much at all. We were both aware the day had been a special one that we would add to the long list of shooting days we have enjoyed together. In our minds was the thought that this

was another one that they couldn't take away from us. I murmured a few words of gratitude and drove away happily into the winter night.

I arrived at another shoot when the snowfall earlier in the week had settled, and there had been a couple of sharp frosts which had embedded it. It was as a result of this that the team assembled in the yard with even more than their usual anticipation. Putting it another way, they were keener than ever.

The familiar briefing, the draw for numbers, and we were away for the first drive, 'The Grasses'. Almost always a productive drive for both pheasants and partridges, I knew that with the wind blowing hard, it would be better than average this morning. It was that. Early on the partridges skimmed along the hedge line that runs through the middle of the drive separating guns five and six, and then rose and curled to find an escape route on the flanks. In most cases it was too late as the buff birds hurtled onwards in the wind to be met with a rattle of shots. Most flew on unscathed, but the odd bird fell to the great satisfaction of the successful gun. Not a big pick up here today.

The next drive was from the Lagoon, a square cover with plenty of bottom to it and with the added benefit of having game cover on two sides. There were early partridges here too, which had been flushed from the back of the drive and I clawed one out of the sky that fell a good 70 yards behind me. On the wind, most of the pheasants favoured a line over the right-hand guns and they had some exciting shooting, with the game really too fast and erratic for them to score heavily.

The speed of the birds in the first two drives was shown up by the next one – Admiral's – where the birds had to fly into the wind and where the guns made a tidy job of shooting them. Although we had a drink next, it wasn't the alcohol that wrecked the cartridge-to-kills ratio of the guns at the Triangle, it was the speed, height and curl in the flight of the birds. This was a fantastic drive with high quality birds aplenty.

The fields were all snow covered and the trees and hedges lined in white. The snow underfoot crackled slightly in the frost that held all day, except where it was challenged most strongly by a weak wintry sun for a couple of hours on the top of the day. For the London-based guns, and there were several, this would likely be their best shooting day of the season. They did not have the luxury, as I did, of shooting mid-week or taking a by day just because the weather looked promising. Their days – at weekends mainly – were pre-booked and so for them the snow and the sun and the sheer majesty of the day were a very special treat.

By lunch time our bag was still small, but no one was in the least bit worried. The host and the keeper had presented plenty of birds. The guns had had their chances and plenty had been missed. Between old friends – and most of these were very old friends – hitting and missing was of no consequence at all. There were no targets to meet, nor any expected bags to achieve. They, and I include myself in this, were just there to enjoy themselves, and were doing just that.

Lunch in the barn, which was a lot of fun but a little long, meant the light was lessening by the time we were on our pegs for the penultimate drive of the day. The sting had gone out of the wind by now, and the guns shot better than they had in the morning. And then, in the dying day, we stood for Church Plantation. My peg was in the historic meadow behind the church and only the ancient railings and the years separated me from several members of my family, whose remains rested there. And I thought, as I took a cock bird curling back on my right and a hen streaking out to my left, that my shots would not disturb their rest. A third bird down in the shrubbery, and a good retrieve for my old dog, and that was the last. I walked up the grassy slope to the Hall and thought that with dog at heel and gun under arm at the end of a shooting day with friends, I was the happiest man in England.

Go Seek! Hi Lost!

That December afternoon, the Highland river was in spate as we roughed up its right bank. Over the years earlier spates had variously shaped and reshaped that bank, rendering it impossible to include it in the grass pasture that was a feature of that part of the strath. Some years previously a stock fence had been erected, and a few hundred yards of bank side had become overgrown with whin, wild raspberries and reeds. We were shooting three guns and had one well forward, another back, and myself in the middle with my spaniels. After a lean morning, we had dropped into some game and shot the odd partridge and pheasant. Both my spaniels were working well and the old dog was keeping up with the young one. Halfway along this stretch of cover, the youngster flushed a woodcock and watched it go back and then make to cross the river. He saw and heard the back gun fire and the 'cock glide into the grass on the far bank.

I sent out the old dog first but he could not cope with the fast-flowing water adjacent to the bank, and returned to me shaking the water from his coat. He was not going to get that bird, so I decided to try the young dog. I took him well downstream – perhaps 80 or 90 yards below where we were. Down there, the river formed a good-looking salmon lie and the pace of the water was less than in the shallower rapids at and above the head of the pool.

Sending the young dog out, he swam across the river with no trouble at all and I started to handle him upstream. All went well until he reached a stock fence that stuck out into the river to prevent stock getting round the end of it in low water. Here, to my surprise, the wee dog took to the water again and swam round the end of the fence. On coming ashore again he pressed on upstream and hunted for and soon retrieved the woodcock.

Never previously a keen or reliable retriever, he carried the woodcock back to the fence, plunged into the river and swam round the end of it and back to the bank. He ran downstream, still gamely holding the bird, and attempted to re-cross. The bow wave he caused as he surged the stream was significant; he was swimming for all he was worth. Even so, he was swept downstream some distance before making it back to me, and delivering the woodcock to hand. As I fussed the dog I marvelled at the task he had just achieved and the guts he had demonstrated in so doing. I thought his was a really creditable effort.

On another day, my old black Labrador, Kaiser William the Second – called 'Two' for short – was with me at the grouse. I can remember we parked by the explosives shed in the old quarry and started what we planned as a roughly circular walk on a cheek wind. Grouse were plentiful and by half past one in the afternoon we had three brace in the bag. Well pleased with that, we

left:
Brought to hand

were grousing back to the place the truck was parked. I was the left of two guns as we hunted the last long shoulder of heathery hillside. Two made like a pointer, racing up and down the slope until, suddenly, he was standing still holding grouse at the bottom of the escarpment and from the look in his eyes their scent must have been extremely strong. Edging level with him, and a few yards above him on higher ground, I was able to look into his glazed eyes. He was high on the scent of grouse.

We – the two guns and the dog – were standing stationary near the base of the hillside where the heather swum in the heat. How long we stood either side of the pointing dog I cannot say, but I can recall quite clearly how we three – men and dog – were poised to strike before the shots that broke the spell immediately after the covey rose.

Then there was that day, three years after the great gale, when the woods were strewn with the wreckage of fallen trees and the brambles had embraced the broken branches. We met at the farm. The guns were a mixed team: a few local farmers, a brace of rough and ready business types and, incongruously, an artist who painted saccharine pictures of birds. I didn't have time for much chat with them, as I needed to give my full attention to my task for the day. I was only there to work Fleck, my hard-going, indefatigable springer spaniel of that era.

above:
Sleepy springers

Fleck came from a keeper's kennels in Cumbria, and was an old-fashioned type of springer spaniel. If he had been a horse, he would have been a cob. He was stocky, with a wide chest and short, strong legs. His head was noble and his coat liver and white with flecks of liver all over the white. He was strong, bold and fearless; he loved to hunt.

First drive was the Road Belt and I kept Fleck at heel. With the strong possibility he might go out on to the road, there was no way I was going to hunt him and risk him being run over by a passing car. A few birds went forward and one or two were shot. I didn't trouble with these but, with the other beaters and dog men – and there were only five of us – I made my way to Lowes Plantation which was, thankfully,

GO SEEK! HI LOST!

drive. It was always a challenge to drive this horseshoe-shaped wood with a small beating team, as too much or too little pressure would result in birds leaking out. When we started, I was on the outside of the horseshoe, where the cover was thickest, and knew my colleagues on my left, having a shorter distance to go, would give me all the time I needed to hunt my right wing.

With tennis court sized patches of bramble growing through fallen timber and branches, Fleck came into his own here. He was giving his work his full attention and I could see and hear the cover snapping and cracking as he hustled and harried the game. Fleck charged into each area of cover and first I would see the bramble almost unzipping as he raced around while hunting the pheasants in it. Then, as he got nearer to the far side of it, birds would break, some running on and others flushing and finding their way forward through the trees.

Fleck was hot to handle now, and it took all my concentration and effort to keep him in check. His excitement in the hunting and mine in the handling matched each other. I liken it to riding a race horse, combining an animal's awesome power and fitness and, for the rider, the fear that he may lose control. I tried to get round each piece of cover to hold Fleck up and calm him down before his next encounter and that day, all day long, I succeeded.

well away from any roads. I let Fleck hunt here and he hustled several pheasants out of the box bushes in which they were hiding. I entered him in each bush separately and kept well up with him to stop him going on. Next, in the Pits, Fleck really came into his own, and I put him to hunt in patch after patch of brambles, some of which were so thick I could not see him. Then I watched for the moving bramble stems and leaves, and used the whistle when I had to maintain control of my hot dog.

We ate our sandwiches in the barn and after eating mine as quickly as I could I slipped away early to dog in what was called the Arthur's Belt. Several pheasants skimmed forward out of this and into the West Wood ready for the start of the

When I stepped out of the West Wood one of the farmers congratulated me on the good show of pheasants that had flown forwards. It was good to know that Fleck's work was appreciated and there was no doubt he was at the top of his game.

There was one more drive and a short one too around the farm yard, thank goodness, as Fleck was tiring. Even so, it was he who charged into the hollies and flushed the last birds of the day. Back at my truck, when I instructed Fleck to jump up into his box, he simply stood, rocking slightly with sheer exhaustion from his work. I picked him up and gently placed him in his box. I took him home, lifted him out again and carried him into his kennel. When I looked in on him an hour later he was asleep, deep down in the straw of his box.

Fleck, bless him, left me many years

ago and he and his hunting are twilight memories now, but I never think back to the shooting times we spent together without hoping that there is some Valhalla where he and I may together hunt our way to that distant horizon where the earth meets the sky.

As always, there was much to do on the morning of my own shoot many miles away in the black fens. I had my habitual list as long as my arm to remind me of every item. I needed to take coffee and drinks, lunch for six, glasses and cups. I needed the radios, spare batteries, string for bracing and hanging the shot game. I put in coats and boots, gun and cartridges. Most important was the bag for my spaniel, Brandy, with his snack and towel and a dry bag for the drive home at the end of the day. I checked I was wearing my whistle and that I had a lead for him during the walk in to the duck jumping manoeuvres. I checked every item off and all the time the old dog followed me around. He was determined not to be left behind!

At last, with Brandy on board in his dog box, I headed into the traffic for a while before picking up the country roads leading into the fens and to my shoot. As always, this was to be a day for guns with dogs, when our sport and our bag would depend heavily on well-controlled spaniel work.

My guest guns turned up at the farm and as they changed from shoes to boots there was a sense of anticipation for today was to be a rare chance for them to test their spaniels to the limit. Old hands, they knew how steep the dykes were and how the scent of pheasants running forward through the sugar beet would send even the best trained dog demented. This was high-risk stuff for these serious spaniel men. This is not the place to re-tell the events of this day at the farm, but to recount Brandy's part in it. As we walked the first field for a chance at the duck on the drain, he hung in at heel. The duck jumped in front of us and I had one down in the water. I sent Brandy, who swam over to the far side and retrieved it from the shallow water before swimming back and climbing the high bank, snuffling in a noisy manner though its breast feathers.

Next I put him to hunt an overgrown bank, a 500-yard stretch of thistles and weeds including fat hen and sweethearts galore. He flushed two pheasants from this cover and hunted out a rabbit lying up in the long grass. One pheasant was bagged; the other went away without offering a shot and the rabbit was missed with both barrels. By the time we all linked up Brandy's coat was matted with burrs.

Next, we tried our usual drive off the lake, at the end of which there were several mallard to pick. Leaving the duck in the water to the Labradors, I worked Brandy in the tall reeds round the edge and he put in a big effort here, having to fight his way through the reeds to reach

above:
Back to master

duck that had drifted in to the edge. I went in with him as far as I could and knocked down reeds to give him channels to go and return by. At length, I decided he had had enough. He's always been a dog that suffers in the wet and I took him back to the farm and towelled him down so that he did not suffer while we had lunch, and also fed him some sweet stuff. This was self-interested as I needed him to hunt strongly during the afternoon.

We went to the sugar beet after we had eaten our piece and here it was possible to watch all the spaniels. Apart from one, they all erred and even Brandy, well old enough to know better, roared away up a wheeling and flushed a cock pheasant that had run on a good 100 yards ahead of us. Having allocated three guns the task of heading the

field, or at least the strip we were shooting at that stage, I was miffed to see that cock go out the side and avoid all the guns as he flew long and low over the farm boundary. After recovering Brandy, I had a few words with him about his misbehaviour but the impression he gave me was that the hunt had been such fun it made enduring any reproof worthwhile.

In the remaining walks Brandy and I were working dykes, reeded and overgrown for the most part, and he worked well. We certainly covered some distance and by mid-afternoon he was hanging at my heel. I looked along the line and saw all the spaniels were similarly subdued. "The dogs are done! Let's give it best," I suggested, and none of my guests demurred.

By the time we had walked back to the

farm Brandy was nearly out on his feet, like a boxer after some long bout. Before I did anything else, I cleaned him up as best I could, bagged him up in his towelling dog bag, and placed him in his box. The day of the springer was done.

Old Brandy sleeps in the boot room at home and, in that night, I went in now and then to check on him. His greeting was a tail wagged quietly as if it hurt to wag it at all, with his deep brown eyes affectionately raised. I knelt down beside him, took his tired old head in my arms and spoke to him with words only the affection of which could he understand. He was, I made plain to him, a dog well beloved.

I was brought up around gun dogs from my early childhood and absorbed the belief of my father and his associates that, if you went shooting, you should keep a dog. My father sometimes recalled a sharp lesson he had on this subject on the occasion of his first 'solo' shooting invitation. Having decided to leave his dog at home in case it let him down, he strapped his shotgun to his bicycle and arrived in good time at the yard of his farmer host. "Got your gun, boy?" enquired the farmer, and when father replied that he had, the next question was, "Have you got your dog, boy?"

Father admitted he had left his dog at home, and was immediately instructed to go back and bring him. He rarely shot without one during his long shooting life.

Father favoured Labradors for their game finding ability, and he was always appreciative of a gun dog with a good nose. By chance, the best gun dog he had was around my teen years, and she was a black Labrador bitch of easy, pliant disposition, and she had a superlative nose. As I often accompanied my father on local shoots, before I started shooting on them myself, I witnessed the many occasions on which she made fine retrieves of pheasants and partridges that would otherwise have been left lingering and lost.

At that time, the picking up industry was in its infancy and guns were expected to have their own dogs. They certainly couldn't expect to have behind the gun line the team of gun dog handlers that is commonplace nowadays. On one occasion, I recall being taken with this dog to a newly-acquired shoot by one of father's military connections, a retired general of some distinction in his day. We did several drives in a big wood – there were no game covers – and on one of these the General winged a hen pheasant which planed down through the trees behind the peg and quickly ran off through the wood. At the end of the drive the General, who had no dog of his own, ordered me to search for his runner, while everyone else went off to the next drive. I was about twelve years old, nervous of handling my father's dog, and awed by being left alone in a large wood I didn't know. Anyway, the bitch had no such scruples. Taken to the fall, she soon picked

up the line of the running bird and followed it with her nose close to the ground. There was no under storey and that hen pheasant had run away fast – I had seen her go with my own eyes – so it was likely she had gone on a long way. I trotted along behind the bitch as she worried the line and, after what seemed like a mile but was probably only a couple of hundred yards, she paused and showed interest in the bole of an ancient oak tree. She tried casting off but kept returning and trying to get into what looked like a rabbit hole in the bottom of this. Going up to it, I spotted two hen pheasant breast feathers and, by inserting my arm, managed to extract the General's runner. I was filled with pride for 'my' dog at this find and no doubt bored the General stiff by telling him all about her virtues.

As I progressed through my early teens, this great bitch was my invariable companion during all my shooting, which ranged from pigeon decoying to rough and driven days for game of all descriptions. I took my dog with me when invited to stay with my school friend in Essex. Among the farmers of that post war era, the possession of a Land Rover and a dog were prerequisites for regular shooting invitations and, although just a lad, I was made to feel very welcome because I had brought my dog.

In that era, except on a few big shoots, game was scarce in comparison with the amount of it there is now, and a lost runner was not just that but also the loss of somebody's supper. Those were pre-foodie times and perhaps greater value was placed on the game shot as it was all destined for someone's pot. In just a few years, by the time I was able to have and keep a gun dog of my own, obtaining picking up places had become quite competitive and I rarely got involved with it. I wanted a gun dog for hunting and retrieving and used, first Labradors, and secondly springer spaniels for the rest of my shooting career.

I made a dreadful mistake with my first Labrador. As so often seems to happen when one wants to buy a puppy, I could not find any litters with working lines and impetuously bought a pup with show dog sire and dam. This puppy was useless and I had to re-home her at a loss. Years later, I got caught again by buying a pup by a dam that a picker up owned and worked, but for which he had no papers. He told me he had acquired the dam from a former gamekeeper who was known to me by name. Some weeks later the seller obtained and produced the pedigree papers and these disclosed show lines. Although the pup had his good points, he was a sore trial out shooting and would, given the slightest chance, go off on his own. One day, while I was shooting in the north of England, he pleased me by sitting steadily through a drive and then retrieving three pheasants. As I walked back to the gun bus, he ran off wilfully into a huge forestry block, ignored the whistle and did not return for nearly half an hour. He had to go, but by then I had invested hours of hard work in training him. While no doubt a few show dogs make good working dogs, the larrikin temperaments of show dogs make the taming of them a bed of nails and best avoided.

I found a rangy Labrador dog best for my robust style of shooting. I acquired a couple of these in succession to each other and, handling them like spaniels, had enormous

fun with them. The first of these was known as 'Two', a dog that I have described in action in an earlier chapter. Two came to me as a reject, a young picking up dog in a picking up team who had not made a retrieve. As soon as he was on his own, he started retrieving and, happily, I found he was in posession of a first-class nose. In the fens, he was ideal as his long legs helped him while he was hunting the dykes and high-topped sugar beet fields. Over the early seasons, Two learnt his trade on the black fen and became canny in his understanding of the escape and evasion tactics fen pheasants adopt to such good effect.

While handling him down there, where I could see everything that was going on, I learned to 'watch the dog' and became adept at spotting when he was likely to flush game. Very few guns watched the dog. When I walked up one of the dykes with a guest gun, I always instructed him to walk 10 yards out and 40 yards ahead of me. Then I said "And watch the dog!"

The gun could not see the dog when he was below the top of the dyke bank but that should have informed him the dog was in a business district where game was likely to be encountered. When the dog showed on the top of the bank, I was watching closely to see how he was behaving. If he was pulling ahead, then I knew he was following a bird, a cock pheasant most likely, that was running on ahead. I would try to stop him or slow him up by using the whistle, but in the last resort I ran after him. Few guest guns stayed alert to these moments of opportunity after the first 50 yards of the walk up and missed chance after chance because they were unready or in the wrong place.

Two had, as I have said, a very good nose, and found numerous runners both when out on my own and on many other shoots. At Lark Hall Farm, I noticed that the most difficult retrieves were those in which a winged bird would glide down and run into the bank of a dyke. Even if Two or one of the other dogs was at hand, such birds would sometimes disappear as if they

had never been there. I spent hours urging the puzzled dogs to hunt for them. It was some years later that I found the reason for this, and even then it was entirely by accident. Shooting elsewhere in the fens I downed and carefully marked a cock bird that ran into a deep, overgrown dyke bank. Trying to look over the edge of the dyke, I slipped in and found myself in water up to my waist, and with my eyes only a little above the water level. A yard along the bank, I saw the tail of a cock pheasant. The bird itself was tucked in under the bank at water level, completely concealed by overhanging grasses. Although my dog had been in the dyke, his chances of scenting and picking that well-concealed bird was slim, as was demonstrated by his failure on it.

From then on, I had no hesitation in giving a fen runner a second barrel while it was on the ground if I got the chance, and no longer discouraged my dogs running in to the fall. I had learned the hard way that a hunt for a fen pheasant is not over until that pheasant is in the game bag.

In addition to running my own rough shoot, I shot on many other shoots with my friends and also worked my dogs in the lines of various local beating teams. I say dogs advisedly because by then the adaptation of my Labradors to a spaniel's role had caused me to conclude I also needed spaniels. The first of these – the doughty Fleck – came from north country

kennels and was a challenging introduction to the breed. Whatever his faults, and he was hard going, Fleck's work rate was praiseworthy and I came to relish the challenge of working him on shoots where there was a lot of game to test myself with the challenge of handling him when he was hot. On one memorable afternoon, on the right-hand side of the Elm Wood drive, he must have flushed 75 pheasants and I never lost him once. That dog had aspirations to hunt and ambitions to flush game from cover; my challenge was to stay with him while he did so. Sometimes I failed and Fleck rioted, and when he did

the most vocal critics were those without dogs. I took little notice of them as most of them had no understanding of dogs and dog work, and knew nothing whatsoever about the thrills and spills of handling a hard-going working gun dog.

With my ever-increasing enthusiasm for shooting over my own dogs, I took to organising rough shooting on what is termed 'marginal ground' in locations such as Devon and Cornwall, Cumbria, and of course in various counties of Scotland. Ideally only shooting four guns, the most enjoyable of these short trips were those in which we were on good walking up ground.

On one visit to north Devon we stayed near Clovelly and spent a long morning on the left bank of the River Tamar. In a variety of cover, which included interesting game-friendly reed beds, we worked the spaniels to good effect for a mixed bag that is the making of such shooting. By then I was absorbed in such sporting shooting days, in which life's essentials seemed to be reduced to dog, whistle, and gun.

A few weeks ago I met one of my erstwhile companions and we revisited those trips. "Do you remember that walk up by the river in Devon?" were his first words. I did; I remembered it very well. With two others, we had walked up reeds, rough grass, and clumps of willow and alder for a mixed bag of game. He had had a diminutive black Labrador bitch then. He and I had also spent a day shooting the fells at Lowther, where the snipe lay far out on the hill and, on flushing with a rasp, would provide possible but difficult shots. We had learned to keep our dogs in while on the open ground, and to only let them hunt for pheasants and rabbits in the bracken. Later, becoming more ambitious, we had taken some high bird days – regular driven shoot days – and tried our skills at serious north country pheasants. We had spent a lot more money, but – in retrospect – what we remembered best was that rough up with our dogs by the river.

Again, in Scotland, some gamekeepers felt we should be forward as standing guns in their impromptu drives. Hard as they worked, and fun though this was, what I liked best was to find a swale, with perhaps scrub bushes and bracken, and let the spaniels work. Great sport was to be had when there was just a smattering of game – here a pheasant, there a woodcock – rather than when every clump held a game bird. There was a place in the west of Scotland I knew, or rather came to know, in which we followed a fault uphill on the right hand side of a ravine. For their safety, we kept the dogs back from the edge. Only when the rise levelled out did we let them hunt it, and we walked far out on to the hill hunting the bracken and the birches in the gully, investigating minor gullies, hollows and knolls with the dogs, now and then flushing woodcock and the occasional snipe. There were no pheasants there. When we had reached the place where the gully opened out and merged with the heather hill, we wheeled round and walked back down its other side. Clumps of birch, patches of bracken, and areas of whin all merited the attention of the dogs. There was hours of shooting to be had there and I remember coming off the hill with the dogs dead beat and ready for bedding. As the cool winter night crept in we turned out our game bags and admired our quarry, and the spaniels grunted in their boxes as they curled up, head between legs, as weary as only working spaniels can be when their work is done.

Men of the Field

I cannot have been more than five years old when Father took me to visit Mr Johns, the then head keeper of the Thurlow estate. We found Johns on his rearing field. I remember a well-built man dressed in tweed plus fours, who was preoccupied with the broody hens and pheasant chicks in the rows of coops and runs. The highlight of this visit was when Johns produced a newly-hatched pheasant chick from the poacher's pocket of his jacket and allowed me to hold it. I think there was some discussion between my father and Johns over the merits of ant eggs for feeding pheasant chicks. At that time there were no pellets, and all the feed for pheasant chicks had to be laboriously prepared by hand. I was greatly impressed by Johns and regret that I have so few other memories of him.

His successors, Ross and then Bebbington, were rather younger men and no doubt better fitted to running an expanding shoot of that scale and size, and to managing up to eight beat keepers. Even as a youngster the difference between Johns' approach to his profession and that of Ross and Bebbington was very obvious. While Johns rode a bicycle with his shotgun strapped to the cross bar, I always remember Bebbington as being in a Land Rover.

In those days the fox did not have the villain status it has since acquired. With wild game still making an important contribution to the bags of many shoots, the stoat was the arch enemy and all keepers

worth their salt operated trap lines. Tunnels were made in banks and other strategic places and much effective use was made of the gin trap, then still legal. Keepers could all squeak stoats and were rarely far from their guns, which were carried as a matter of course.

I was fascinated by all those gamekeepers; however they carried on their business. Johns impressed me because he seemed such a quiet, reassuring man and so in sympathy with nature. The identification and subsequent elimination of the hedgehog in the Vicarage grounds by Ross impressed me as a smart bit of work. Another beat keeper on the estate was a man called Jack Ivens and he lived in a remote cottage in the woods on his beat. He was of the same generation as Johns and was a man who gave the impression of being perfectly in tune with nature. A lightweight man, Bill Middleton, also lived in a remote cottage which then did not have any services such as mains water, sewerage or electric light. Bill kept ferrets, little jills I remember, and introduced me to ferreting.

Locally, senior keepers had considerable status and none more so then than one Jim Cook. A very bent and gnarled old man at the time I remember him, he was still the gamekeeper on the Gt. Bradley estate. He would meet the guns on a shoot morning on a track close to his home, and I can recall him lurking there with gun and his game bag, which by half nine in

opposite:
The retired keeper

right:
*Bag fillers: cocks and
a red leg*

152

the morning already had the tail feathers of two cock pheasants sticking out of the top. Jim was a very good shot. One day the guns were walking in line through a field of kale. A cock pheasant broke back and was inexplicably missed with both barrels by Major Philip Dawson, a celebrated top shot of those days. The gun to the left of the Major also had two ineffectual shots and it was thought the cock had escaped. Not so! The next gun was Jim Cook, and he killed it stone dead "a mile behind the line". This astounding shot was talked about for years and it was ironic that so gifted a game shot as Major Dawson should have been remembered as the victim of Jim Cook's amazing eye wipe rather than for his many fine feats with his gun.

In the times I am talking about – the 1950s and 60s – local shoots were just that. Although occasional guns were visitors from London or elsewhere, most were local. Almost all the beaters were villagers, and some of these were considerable characters.

I have already mentioned some of the great characters among the guns in that era. There were the local farmers, some gallant men and others who had worked in agriculture during the war. There was the tweed suit brigade of retired military men, and I much regret I was too young to find out about the experiences they had had and the dangers they had survived. Subsequently, after his death, I was to read an account of Major-General Gregson's part in the Battle

of Keren, when he was a young 'Bimbashi' – an Indian Army subaltern. Brigadier Frink had, I believe, been in the thick of things in the Battle of Arakan in Burma and, although I spent time with him as a child, he never mentioned what had happened. Geoffrey Scoones, an unremarkable old gentleman, was of course the formidable General Scoones of the same Burma war and I can only say in my own defence that in old age he was so mild mannered one would never have known it.

At my young age all that mattered to me was that these were men of the field, and I admired them for their exploits in that and for their kindness and encouragement towards myself as a small boy. It was Kid Dennis, one of father's great friends, who took me fly fishing for rudd on his farm pond. It was 'Frinky' who gave me my first fishing rod, which I used to great effect against the roach in a local ornamental canal. The canal belonged to a delightful old gentleman Major James, but always called 'Jim', Bartholomew, who allowed me to fish it. Jim was a First World War veteran but never spoke of his experiences. These men and many more fanned the flames of my enthusiasm for fieldsports so that I too became a man of the field.

For younger readers, or for those who have come to shooting more recently, it may be difficult to grasp how much more local game shooting was then and how there was, in the aftermath of war, much more make do and mend. Certainly, the gamekeepers, beaters and guns of today's shoots cut a very different dash to those of 50 years ago. Fortunately, neither the intervening years nor today's shooting world have been devoid of their characters.

I once met the late George Wilson, for many years Lord Lambton's head keeper at Lambton Park, which was then in the process of being engulfed by the conurbations of Newcastle and Durham. Charged with maintaining a very heavy pheasant shoot and a game farm in the park, Wilson had his work cut out to deter poaching, theft and vandalism on an industrial scale. On one occasion he was shot at by night poachers, and his response to this was to buy an awesome black German shepherd dog called Sultan. Such a terrible reputation did this dog establish in the North East that an announcement through Wilson's loud hailer that Sultan was being sent into a wood was often enough to induce night poachers to surrender and come out quietly. Wilson took no nonsense from anyone. Encountering two youths trespassing on scooters in the park, they gave him lip. He ran over the scooters and destroyed them. He then picked up each youth by the back of the neck and the seat of the trousers and threw them into the back of his Land Rover. An eyewitness reported that the heads made an awful sound when they hit the steel panel dividing the front from the back. Both youths were taken to the local police station and pulled out by their feet on to the road for the attention of the duty sergeant.

After chasing a trespassing girl through the park, Wilson was heard to comment that when he had caught her he couldn't remember why he had wanted to catch her.

Briefing an overly-enthusiastic new employee of the late Lord Lambton, Wilson cautioned him against thinking His Lordship was nice all the time. "Look out for when he starts kicking stones," he counselled, "and when he does, get the f*** out of it!"

Wilson's shoot days in Lambton Park were famous not just for the number of birds and the height at which they flew, but for his conduct of proceedings. In a major drive such as Hedworth's, pheasants would be flying over the guns for over an hour, and in all that time not so much as a tap or a voice would be heard from the beating line. The silence of the beating team was awesome.

The money and resources poured into some modern shoots equals or exceeds those of the big shoots of Edwardian England. Such shoots require positive leadership and man management skills which, in turn, are provided by some very able head keepers. Such men must have many skills and attributes among which the role of man of the field is only one. They are, after all, managing budgets of hundreds of thousands of pounds a year. Their sophisticated management skills, knowledge of the law,

opposite:
The gun

and ways of going to work are a far cry from Mr Johns working hard and single-handedly on his rearing field, and keeping an eye out for a rogue stoat. Some of these gamekeepers have become involved in shoot management themselves and, being in the best way obsessed with shooting, have operated their own distinctive and highly successful shoots.

One such is Richard Clarke, who went to Six Mile Bottom estate to develop a partridge shoot for Enterprise Oil on land that had become infested by unsavoury packs of long dog men and other louts, who roamed it at will and unopposed. His experiences in so doing would fill a book on their own. Suffice to say here, when that company was taken over Clarke took on the lease and operated the shoot successfully for several years. Although the days were too heavy for my personal taste, he put on some spectacular shooting, particularly for partridges on the wide open spaces of that estate. Clarke had, and has, great ability as a driver of partridges and, on a day with a decent breeze, a drive such as Daddy's Bush would be one every gun would wish to

shoot. It's a shame his lease expired as, since he has moved on to be Mine Host at the Green Man in Six Mile Bottom, that shoot has just not been the same. I have heard Clarke criticised for putting on excessively large days, but the fact remains he has introduced literally hundreds of people to game shooting and done more to make the sport popular than those who complain about his bags.

Some landowners regard their shoots solely as a source of income and try to maximise this, while giving as little help as possible to the shoot and those connected with it. I have shot on shoots where even the guns are made to feel that they are not wanted, and are just allowed there on sufferance to help provide funds for the estate. Needless to say I did not return to such shoots. The best shoots are those in which conservation is the watchword and shooting the objective.

On other estates, the representatives of farm management companies can be really unhelpful, and some of them appear to be almost manic in their pursuit of agri-profit. As these managers are not part of the estate, they tend to operate their machinery without any regard or consideration for the shoot, particularly while combining and harvesting root crops at night. They ignore the fact that the shoot frequently provides a useful income stream for the estate. Where a heavy rent is paid and the shoot is charged heavily for game covers and grain for feed, the overheads of the shoot can become quite alarming. When this happens, as it does time and again, it is the gamekeeper who has to hold the dirty end of the stick. Any number of examples of the way things have gone – and not for the better in my opinion – are illustrated on estates all over the country. 50 years ago, the owners would have operated low-key syndicates which enjoyed 10 or a dozen days a season. They were shooting men who shot with their syndicate. Now, with more non-shooting owners, there are estates on which in excess of 30 days of shooting take place each season on the same ground. These days are necessary to balance the books.

I feel much sympathy for the long-suffering gamekeepers and their wives, who not only have a full shooting season from September to February to manage, but also have a rearing programme commensurate with the large amount of shooting that takes place. One might be forgiven for thinking that the rent charged is for the farm land, not just the shoot. So many gamekeeper husband and wife teams must put on all these days in a professional way and with good humour, but are asked to do far more than is reasonable or fair in order to balance the books. Although some might argue that today's syndicates should not take the shoot if the rent is too high, I do not accept this argument. They often feel a responsibility to the gamekeeper and his wife, who have provided great sporting shooting for them and their predecessors. As, in effect, trustees of the shoot, they would be loath to walk away from it and see it disbanded.

It is not just high rents that are a threat to the viability of shoots, and nor is it such obvious enemies such as the fox or stoat. In my view, the greatest threat is public access. Today's gamekeeper has to have all sorts of qualities to manage this, and the problems it throws up in connection with game conservation.

The official line of the shooting organisations is that shooting people should be very gentle with trespassers. While this is good in principle, the behaviour of the public at large beggars belief. I have lost count of the number of times I have stopped someone with a rioting dog in the spring time and have had my request that they return to the nearest public footpath answered with the words: "Let's be reasonable!" With the trespasser's dog roaring around in cover occupied by my nesting game, there is little incentive for me to be reasonable.

On another occasion a woman started walking two collies all over a shoot with which I was involved. One morning, I was parked in my truck at the end of a conservation strip and spoke to her, pointing out that she had no business be on it and that she should use the adjacent footpath. She was stroppy, but eventually went on her way. That same evening her husband was found walking the two dogs off the path and, when challenged, he complained that his wife had already encountered a rude man who had 'pointed his gun at her' which had been reported to the police. I was that man, so it was fortunate another local gamekeeper was sitting in the passenger seat of my truck during the conversation and could vouch for the fact that throughout it both our rifles were hidden out of sight within my truck.

My experience is that members of the public who trespass will tell any old lie in order to excuse themselves. These range from having permission from the farm manager to being related to someone who worked on the estate years previously. My gamekeeper friend, Scurry, erects signs on all his conservation strips in terms that should prevent people walking them, but some walkers are shameless. In his experience the women are worse than the men, and not unusually resort to abusive language when they are challenged. On one occasion, Scurry came on a man walking through the middle of a field of ripe barley. When Scurry pointed out the was trampling the barley, this man produced £25 in notes from his back pocket and proffered it in compensation on the basis that such a sum would more than reimburse the damage he was doing to the crop.

Another obnoxious man habitually walked his terriers through Scurry's game covers and, when challenged, variously offered to fight him and abused him as "a rural idiot". When threatened with a court injunction, he turned out to be a bull frog and signed an undertaking not to walk off the footpaths again.

One only has to watch well-walked footpaths to appreciate the overwhelming nature of the public access problem. On some paths there is a constant stream of walkers, and for every one of these that stays on the footpath and keeps their dogs on leads, there are always others who go off path and let their dogs run wild hundreds of yards around them.

Today's gamekeepers and shoot operators have to have remarkable diplomatic skills in minimising the damage that these people do, but there must be many times when they would like to resort to some traditional Anglo Saxon language.

During my shooting career it is not just trespassing walkers who have disturbed my game. On occasion, shooting neighbours have been the culprits. For a time, on my fen shoot, my neighbour kept a game cover in and adjacent to mine – up against the boundary – and his gamekeeper took to dogging out my adjoining land on a daily basis. He was an uncouth fellow, but stopped when challenged about it.

There were others, but none of them was such a pain in the neck as 'Zorba', who had the shoot next to mine for some years. Zorba's land was ideal for holding and showing pheasants, having a mixture of low ground and slopes and some woodland with excellent habitat. Zorba reared pheasants for his commercial shoot.

In contrast, my shoot was a social affair involving family and friends. There were some drives from small blocks of game cover and others from woods and hills. One of our woods divided two of our fields adjacent to Zorba's land. This appeared to have the potential of a good drive but on the day invariably disappointed. There were very few birds in it.

One morning, on making ready to shoot it, I found Zorba on the boundary with two dogs. He was in his ground so I said good morning to him and started the drive. There was just one cock pheasant in it. "I thought on that" as we say in the countryside, and eventually caught Zorba in my wood dogging the game in it towards his land.

There was a very distasteful follow-up, with denials by Zorba that he was hunting out the belt, claims that he had permission to do so, apologies for having done so, and offers to lease the shooting rights over the wood.

Needless to say, I would have nothing to do with these increasingly desperate solutions. In the end, under the threat of court proceedings for an injunction and damages, Zorba promised never again to enter my wood and field. Time will tell whether he honours his undertaking.

Zorba was seemingly quite incapable of grasping that my pheasants, released on the top of the hill, would always be prone to wandering downhill into his domain and that it was therefore in his interests to have me rear and release as many as possible. In his warped mind, all the pheasants on our ground were his pheasants. I was disgusted by his unneighbourly and unsporting behaviour, and by the illegality of his actions.

A Mixed Bag

Such of my readers as have read shooting books published in the last century will no doubt have noticed at least two huge differences between then and now. In bygone times there was virtually no mention of the law relating to firearms and shooting. Now there is often detailed advice and information on this subject. In the old days there was no concern about the future of shooting. In our times, firearms ownership and shooting are under relentless attack.

During my career as a solicitor I represented many clients in firearms act appeals. These clients were usually firearms and shotgun certificate holders who had variously been refused applications for the grant or renewal of one or both of these certificates, or had suffered the revocation of them for some perceived misdemeanour. Subsequent to my retirement as a solicitor, my company Shootinglaw Ltd. has supplied, and continues to supply, detailed legal advice to such people. My experience in this field has led me to certain conclusions as to the conduct of firearms licensing.

Firstly, the present system is wasteful of resources. The five-year duration of certificates and the renewal work this entails is expensive and serves little useful purpose. Secondly, police licensing departments are, with honourable exceptions, prone to a combination of risk aversion and social correctness. Thirdly, they are supported in this by the unfairness of the appeal system. By way of example, it is apparent that in many cases an unhappy wife or girlfriend only has to call the police, complain of domestic violence and mention that 'he has a gun', to instigate a raid by armed police officers and the revocation of the holder's certificates. The police are thereby seen to be having a zero-tolerance policy towards domestic violence and towards public safety, and can also record a call out to a 'firearms related' incident.

They are supported in this by the high cost of firearms act appeals and the current law, which habitually prevents successful appellants recovering their costs in these appeals while making them liable for the police costs should their appeals be refused. To this injustice should be added the legal authority of the 'Kavanagh' case, which enables the crown court to admit hearsay evidence – i.e. gossip – and attach such weight to that hearsay evidence as, in its discretion, it thinks fit. I know of several cases in which the unfortunate certificate holder has been the subject of maliciously motivated and unfounded complaints by his spouse or partner and has had his certificates revoked. On his appeal, the police have not even called the complainant wife or girlfriend, and have simply put in and relied on her statement of evidence to further blacken a good name. Nor do I say this lightly. Certificate holders have to be of good character to hold their certificates and are subject to a wide range of checks

opposite:
Roe: a snow doe

and enquiries on grant and renewal. The unsatisfactory manner in which certificate holders are refused and revoked for extraneous matters unrelated to firearms is discriminatory and unfair. No other section of society is subject to such sanctions, at either the ground floor licensing level or on appeal.

I am well placed to support these observations from the portfolio of unreported cases in which Shootinglaw and myself have advised. The head notes relating to a few of them may help keep certificate holders out of trouble.

Mr A had had a long-term and admittedly lively relationship with a volatile female. After the breakdown of this, she refused to repay a substantial amount of money that she owed him. He pressed for repayment. In response, she made complaints to the police about Mr A's behaviour. These included allegations that he had guns and had threatened to use them against her.

Mr A's shotgun certificate was revoked as a result of this false and malicious complaint. On appeal, he was successful and his certificate eventually returned to him.

Mr B had a spat outside his house with an obnoxious cyclist who was obstructing the highway, which the cyclist filmed and recorded on his mobile phone. Based on what the police and firearms department saw on the film, which only showed half the incident, Mr B had his certificates revoked.

right:
SSSIs like listed buildings

He appealed and, in the course of preparing for the appeal, it transpired that the cyclist had been embroiled in arguments and rows with other residents who lived in the same street as Mr B. These residents made statements in support of Mr B's appeal and after months of deprivation and worry, Mr B's certificates were returned to him.

Mr C was standing by his vehicle, which contained his concealed shotgun, when it was stolen from under his nose. He had stopped briefly beside a main road when a man jumped out of a passing car and took and drove it away – an unlikely and audacious theft if ever there was one. The vehicle was fortunately recovered with the shotgun still inside it. However, Mr C was still revoked for breach of standard condition 4(c) of his shotgun certificate and had to issue an appeal notice and appear in the crown court when, happily, his appeal succeeded. Mr B and Mr C were, I should add, the keenest of shooting men and had they been permanently deprived of their certificates, they would have found this a life-changing event.

Having suffered a bad year due to a combination of a family bereavement and work issues, Mr D consulted his family doctor, who prescribed a course of mild anti-depressant tablets. He took a couple, before discarding this remedy. On the renewal of his shotgun certificate he very properly disclosed the consultation and, in consequence, had his application for renewal refused. Being unable to fund an appeal he reluctantly had to accept this decision.

The blameless Mr E lived next door to some 'neighbours from hell' and had not infrequently to report their activities to the local police. Eventually, Mr E's certificate was revoked on the basis that, having such provocative neighbours, he could not possess a shotgun without danger to the public or the peace.

Mr F was a gamekeeper who had several altercations with a persistent trespasser – a woman who walked where she wished and let or encouraged her dogs to hunt out his game covers and woodland. She made complaints to the police that he had threatened her and had pointed his gun at her. Mr F only escaped revocation by fortunately having a respectable witness of good character with him at the time of the relevant encounter. As it was, he was interviewed under caution.

Another sad case I recall concerned Mr G, who was a well-regarded citizen in his rural neck of the woods, a family man in his late 60s. Mr G had recently become interested in shooting and applied for a shotgun certificate. In completing the application form he declared that he had had no previous convictions. This was untrue as, 40 years previously, while living in London, he had been convicted of armed robbery and sentenced to a term of hard labour in Dartmoor Prison. In his subsequent fresh

start in the country, and in his marriage and role as a respectable family man, he had never mentioned or disclosed his past. Mr G was now prosecuted and convicted of making a false statement in his application, which conviction was splashed across the local press wrecking both his local reputation and his family life. Although by the letter of the law correctly convicted – indeed Mr G pleaded guilty to the criminal charge against him – I felt great sympathy for him and was saddened to learn that he died shortly afterwards.

Mr H came to the notice of the police as a result of drink driving. He had two convictions within 10 years and, although in both of these cases the excess alcohol recording was only marginally over the limit, the second conviction caused his chief constable, relying on the well known case of 'Germain v The Chief Constable of Essex', to revoke his certificate. Much use is made of this 'Germain' case by police licensing authorities when considering the revocation of or refusal to grant certificates in the case of persons who allegedly have an intemperate lifestyle. While this approach may be sensible if applied with common sense, there is an erroneous current tendency to apply it too strictly, so that any high-spirited certificate holder who likes a glass or three is classed as a danger to the public or the peace and deprived of his firearms.

In no other area is the behaviour of the participant unrelated to his preferred activity (in this case firearms ownership and use) so rigorously examined. So, for example, many licensed drivers are on the roads in spite of colourful lifestyles that would routinely debar them from being a shotgun or firearms certificate holder. With the pressure now placed on certificate holders through some current approaches to firearms licensing, one must harbour suspicions as to the agenda of those responsible for it. The present treatment of a generally law abiding section of the community – if not the most law abiding – leaves a lot to be desired and legislation is required to remedy it. With today's urban-orientated government, redress is unlikely to be a priority.

The firearms law licensing authorities are sadly not alone in their abuse of members of the shooting community. The conduct of the RSPB, particularly in relation to upland gamekeepers and landowners, simply beggars belief. In its fanatical opposition to shooting, the RSPB ignores the good conservation work that upland gamekeepers do. It is in denial as to benefits of predator control. Instead, it focuses on

and pours resources into the investigation and prosecution of so-called 'wildlife crime'. A realistic assessment would acknowledge there will always be a few cases of this, just as there are of any other category of crime, but sadly there is no realism, only a continuous, crude mud-throwing campaign to demean the dignity and diminish the respectability of gamekeeping, which is one of the countryside's most important professions.

As to the conduct of some of the enquiries into alleged cases of 'wildlife crime', those responsible in the RSPB and the police should be ashamed of themselves. Their treatment of the suspected individuals has in these cases been way over the top, and out of all proportion to the importance and gravitas of the offences for which they were being investigated. In one case, the dawn raid on a gamekeeper's home saw his elderly wife being prohibited from using her own toilet alone. She was watched as she urinated. In another case, the gamekeeper was interviewed in the police station and released on police bail. 15 months passed without him hearing another word. He had not been notified of further action or of a discontinuance of the enquiry. He had simply been left to stew in uncertainty without even any clear notification of the matters against him.

Natural England, as it is now, is another organisation with a record that does not withstand prolonged scrutiny. It is, of course, quite wrongly at one and the same time the promoter and prosecutor of conservation. It is both the educator and enforcer. 'The Nature Police', as some of my clients call it, has vested in it powers more akin to a police state than a democracy.

I recall one case in which Natural England opened proceedings by reporting a landowner to the police for trapping certain mammals, which he was not doing at all. The case collapsed after the usual expense and worry for the individual without a word of regret or remorse from Natural England. It transpired they had only brought the case to avoid paying him annual compensation for profits foregone, and in the fallout from the failed prosecution they were compelled to do this. Subsequently, Natural England tried to avoid the compensation by applying for arbitration, which step they took without any attempt whatsoever to negotiate with the landowner, as would be routine between commercial organisations and individuals. I remember the arbitration that followed for the particularly dysfunctional representatives of Natural England and the relentless financial pressure piled on the farmer landowner. It was a huge relief when the case went his way, and the arbitrator ordered Natural England to pay a six-figure cheque for costs.

Since then I have read and heard of others, such as the Wemmergil grouse moor prosecution in which costs running into hundreds of thousands of pounds were claimed. Then there was the Farndale case, in which Natural England's complaints about damage to a Site of Special Scientific Interest included an allegation that the defendant's pheasants had caused a tree to blow down. The activities complained of there were, I believe, being carried on largely if not wholly outside the boundary of the SSSI designated land.

In contrast to these oppressive complaints and prosecutions against often constructive and creative landowners and shoot operators, one can but raise an eyebrow over the laissez-faire attitude of Scottish National Heritage – Scotland's equivalent to Natural England. To cite just one case, SNH has allowed the Scottish Forestry Authority to clear fell and trash the slopes rising above the famous River Borgie by the brutal application of heavy machinery in wet weather, clear felling from the dark ages at its very worst. That this river, famed for both its salmon and for fresh water mussels, and of course an SSSI, and has been invested with silt and peat from the hillsides, has made no difference at all. Nor, one supposes, has the fact that the Scottish Forestry Authority and SNH share offices in Edinburgh.

The organisations mentioned above are either government backed or, in the case of the RSPB, a charitable institution. None of them should be politically motivated. However, the way they conduct themselves raises the question, in each case, whether the shooting community can do business with them. Instead of bending over backwards to work with them, it is surely time to consider going on to the front foot and showing them up for what they are. If this means in any particular case discrediting them, then so be it.

The second difference between shooting books of the last century and those of today is the increase and impact of public access. Whereas in the 19th century the facts of the well-known legal case of 'Harrison v The Duke of Rutland' may have been the subject of some amusement – Harrison being taken to court after persistently walking in front of the Duke's grouse butts with a large, brightly coloured, raised umbrella – public access is no joke now. The public and their dogs are prone to walking where they like when they like, with complete disregard for private property rights. The disturbance to nesting game and other wildlife can be massive, as of course it can to reared game.

Although a minority of these trespassers may be against shooting and private land ownership, I believe the majority of them are merely ignorant. They walk where they wish because they do not know they are disturbing any wildlife. They let their dogs run and chase because the dog wants to run and chase. Most of these individuals are exercising in the countryside because it is there, not because they really appreciate it. Many that I observe discreetly walk or run while listening to music or using their mobiles; they have no empathy whatsoever with nature.

Although the so-called right to roam does not apply to cultivated land, the culture of the legislation introduced by the last socialist government has aggravated the problems caused by unauthorised access, and is making the job of the gamekeeper more difficult than it ever was. The law protecting private land ownership needs to be amended to address this, but no gamekeeper or landowner should hold his breath in expectation that this will happen.

Against this negative and destructive backdrop, it's truly amazing that so many good shoots are carried on and conducted with such success, and continue to bring so much employment, enjoyment and pleasure to so many people. If the 'shooting industry', and I use the term here deliberately, could only publicise the conservation, employment and financial benefits that accrue to the UK through shooting, it would do a great deal to neutralise the negative image the pursuit has among the general and mainly urban public. Our shoots should be a subject of celebration and pride, and those that are top drawer should be feted in the same way as are premier division clubs. In the rest of this chapter I would like to contribute my impressions of a few of these shoots, some celebrated and famous, and others unknown outside the small circle of those involved in them.

One such shoot is Belvoir Castle, where I

© Nancy

was privileged to shoot earlier this season, and my book would be incomplete without a description of the whole Belvoir experience. I would explain I was invited to join a team for a celebration shoot on the occasion of a significant event in a great friend's life. This wonderful invitation included an overnight stay in the castle itself. Arriving at six in the afternoon my wife and I were met by a team of underkeepers, in their estate tweeds after a shooting day. One of these introduced himself, secured my gun, and carried our two heaviest bags through the castle to our room. It was worth coming for this walk alone, as we passed the numerous antique firearms in the entrance hall and garden room, and then gazed in amazement at portrait after portrait above the stairs and on the walls of the numerous public rooms.

Our room and its en-suite bathroom were really luxurious, and we changed and went down to the library for drinks to find an under butler waiting to look after us. The ambience of this huge, high-ceilinged library with ancient tomes from top to bottom was perfect and particularly appreciated by my wife and myself, both of us keen bibliophiles. There, in that beautiful room, with its books and warming log fire, the team and their wives foregathered for pre-dinner drinks. That and the subsequent dinner in the duke's private dining room made a perfect setting for our celebrations.

Excellent as all this was, our shoot the next day capped it. We were briefed after breakfast by the competent and congenial Mr Phil Burt and conveyed to the first drive in a splendid, liveried Belvoir Castle

above:
Belvoir: High-flying sport

shoot bus. Here the guns were lined out in a valley bottom facing a substantial high bank. There was a stiff left to right breeze here, and it was plain the keeper's plan was to fly the game into this and have them roll back over the gun line. This worked spectacularly for the higher number guns but, with the wind stiffening during the drive, pegs one to four had a thin time.

By good luck, I had drawn number eight and was downwind of all the other guns. Warned to be on the lookout for early partridges, I was delighted to kill the first one that came my way, when it offered me a left to right crossing shot in front. Inevitably, in my position at the bottom of the wind, I had the best of the shooting as the birds that reached me were by and large too good for the guns upwind of me. By the time the drive end whistle went I had enjoyed a great stand, firing more cartridges than I often do in a whole day, and had shot reasonably well by my standards. My peg was on the edge of a stand of trees, and I thought this helped me by giving me some perspective in engaging these high, fast pheasants and partridges.

Any confidence engendered by my bag at the first drive was soon to be dispelled by the birds presented at the second. Here, the guns were placed in a semicircle towards the bottom of a steep grass pasture with a wood behind and somewhat below them. The contour was awesome, and it was obvious that any birds flying over the gun line would be high and likely curling. And so they were; they were truly difficult. The guns on the hot pegs here did well, shooting more than I would ever have done. Even so, a good number of these superbly presented pheasants flew on unscathed. In the course of the drive, a fine Belvoir dog fox appeared, making a pretty picture as he stole unhurriedly alongside a hedgerow and then across some short grass pasture through the gun line. With the historic Belvoir Hunt Kennels less than a mile away, one could say of him that if ever a fox lived in hunt country it was him.

From this drive we were driven to a recently restored pleasure garden area of the estate. Here was a fine octagonal pavilion with terraced decking beside a lake, a pleasant place even on an early December day. Here, in the vicinity of the brazier's warming flames, drinks and eats were served, again with effortless good manners and style. I think it was here I learned that Belvoir Castle puts on in the order of 130 shoot days each year. Although not all of these teams stay overnight in the castle, a very large staff is required to look after the guns and run the shoot days, and nothing is spared in this respect.

After our break, we walked through some well-kept woodland and were dropped off in a wide ride, with the birds expected off the wooded hill opposite. This, it was mentioned, was to be the first woodland pheasant drive of the season. It was a long

drive, which again impressed those of us used to more modest shooting with the quantity and quality of the birds. For some reason the birds were not easy to 'find', and although there was nothing out of shot, my own cartridge-to-kill ratio was poor. However, those that I caught up with gave me great satisfaction.

After a light lunch break, served by more smiling, cheerful staff in an outlying barn, we were taken to what proved arguably to be the best and final drive of the day. Again the guns were placed in a shallow semicircle, this time facing a field of maize on a gentle slope in front of them. The beaters slowly converged on this from the surrounding arable fields and were preceded by the first partridges, which flew over the skyline towards the guns like grouse. As the drive

went on, pheasants also flushed and took the gun line high, fast, and on the curl.

This drive was managed in a masterly way, and it unfolded before the happy guns, who had truly sporting, testing shooting off and on for at least an hour. As my little cocker dog, Midge, busied himself with far more retrieving opportunities than he ever has at home, I thought on the superb day we had enjoyed and all the work that had gone into giving our party a really wonderful experience. I should add it did not end there, as we were taken to the Belvoir Hunt kennels on the way back to lunch at the castle and given a fascinating tour by the huntsman. The kennels were built hundreds of years ago, and are a living reminder of the sporting legacy bequeathed to us by hunting dukes and their hunter associates of many generations.

We finished our day with drinks and a late lunch in another part of the castle with, once again, friendly and immaculate service. The highly trained and obliging Belvoir team make a living from their employment at Belvoir Castle, and it is chilling to think of the damaging effect on the local people so engaged were they not required to provide and service the shooting days every season. A prohibition or continental-style restriction on the releasing of game, for example, could at a stroke effectively wreck this business. So I would say Belvoir Shoot is one that should be praised to the skies and promoted to those politicians, opinion formers, and their fellow travellers until they realise the benefits, economic and otherwise, to the local economy.

As Belvoir Castle is a premier division pheasant and partridge shoot, so Wemmergil leads the same division for grouse. Although the terrain of these low and high ground shoots is of course entirely different, they have one feature in common: the quality and quantity of their staffing.

I was privileged to shoot at Wemmergil in September 2007. A day there enabled me to see that the moor was highly managed. The heather was at different stages, varying from recently burnt to long, so that the grouse had areas for feeding and areas for cover from predators. The extent and amount of this management obviously required a big, well-trained team, and it was obvious that this was in place and working well. For every day's shooting at Wemmergil there must have been many man hours investing in draining, gritting, predator control, and other good gamekeeping practices.

The same attention to detail and high level of investment was to be found in all other aspects of the moor. The butts were well constructed, the tracks properly drained and maintained, and the lunch hut well appointed. Subject to the vagaries of the Pennine weather, I formed the impression that everything that could be done to give the guns a good day had been done. As it happened, on the day I shot there, fog on the higher ground precluded shooting up there until the afternoon, and until then restricted our day to the lower ground of the moor. This was a reminder that in such a hostile environment there are many days when burning and other activities are simply not possible because of bad weather. These are days lost to the moor management.

Once again, when one looks at Wemmergil and grouse moors of that quality and importance, the benefits to the local and national economy are obvious. Wemmergil is situated in an area in which there is little employment – indeed at first blush it appears to comprise inhospitable and uninhabited bleak upland – and so is an important local employer. Wemmergil

above:
Wintering roe in hard times

employs not only gamekeepers, but others in various capacities such as local tradesmen, beaters, flankers and domestic staff. This applies, in degrees, to the many lesser grouse moors in the UK. While it seems perfectly obvious to me that this unique bird and the sport of shooting it should be encouraged and promoted in every possible way, this is not the case. Fuelled by dogma, single-issue focus and class envy, and maybe an irresistible tendency to interfere, government, either directly through legislation or indirectly via agencies such as Natural England, does little to recognise the importance of the industry and much to make its practical operation awkward.

That good moorland gamekeeping enormously benefits other upland hill nesting birds is well known, although only grudgingly acknowledged by the usual culprits. However, good low ground gamekeeping and game conservation also benefits many other birds and mammals. In occasional visits to woodlands managed by wildlife trusts and the like, my impression has been of a lack of wildlife. This may be partly the result of the extensive use of these sites by the visiting public. However, the most significant reason is undoubtedly the absence of any predator control. These well-meaning organisations don't manage wildlife sanctuaries; rather, they create and maintain havens for predators.

The only exception to this non-interventionist, laissez-faire approach appears to be, strangely enough, in relation to deer. My experience of wildlife managers is that they have an obsessive dislike of deer in their woodlands. I am not talking here of a managed population, but of any deer at all. I find it beyond belief that a 'green' enthusiast for nightingales and wood larks can be so singly-focused that he or she cannot tolerate any deer at all in a nature reserve, but this is indeed sometimes the case.

Not long ago, I attended a meeting arranged for local deerstalkers by a local wildlife trust. In the course of an interesting evening, mainly devoted to the habitat and habits of the great crested newt, several learned, science-based explanations of wildlife management were imparted to us but the subject of deer was only mentioned as we left. The organiser's parting words were: 'Have a big cull!' This wholly inappropriate incitement to kill deer was addressed to stalkers from different parts of their county, with different species and numbers of deer on their ground, and quite different and varied cull requirements.

As a result of the deer phobia now prevalent in such organisations and in government departments like DEFRA, there is again a scarcity of some deer species. Roe deer, with their fondness for routine and a small home territory, are particularly vulnerable to excessive, thoughtless culling and to deer poaching.

Once again, it's usually on well-keepered land that deer thrive. Protected from poaching and the stress caused by heavy-handed mass culls, it's on these patches that reasonably numbered populations are to be found. In balance with other activities and managed land, these beautiful animals are an enormous asset. They provide a lovely spectacle, sport for the stalker, and food for the table. In limited numbers the damage they do is tolerable.

Over the years I have stalked deer, I have derived great pleasure from visiting shoots out of the shooting season. I recall magical May mornings on Dava Moor near Grantown-on-Spey, where the curlew and other hill birds wheeled endlessly over the heather hill as they called. There, the roe bucks were very sharp and so much as a scrape of a boot on burnt heather stalks would clear the hill. Corglass, with its black cock lek, was like a giant outdoor cinema screen as we watched the black cock and grey hens at their mating rituals. It was there I shot the 'sleeping buck', which was so old he never moved when we approached him wrong for the wind. In Norfolk, during one roe rut, I sat out a summer downpour while a roe buck and doe mated in the pouring rain and, when it finished, watched the English partridges come out on to the tracks to dry. Near my home in Suffolk, I have watched muntjac come out behind a keeper to scoff the wheat off his feed ride, and watched fallow deer watching passing persons, while waiting to come out for an evening feed on the drilled wheat. All these experiences have occurred on keepered land.

I cannot believe anyone with the slightest interest in the natural world could fail to see the innate beauty of deer of all species. My hope is that in all forms of wildlife management, a more balanced, holistic approach becomes fashionable. Government and the big 'nature' charities need to look at the benefits that derive from nature conservation instead of attacking and undermining it.

Thanks So Much!

Receiving a shooting invitation has always made my day. I have relished the rare early ones that arrive in, say, April, a full six months ahead of the shoot. I have liked those which trickle in during the early summer and then flood in (if I am lucky) in August and September so that the pages of the dairy fill up with reminders such as "Shoot Smith" or "Shoot Jones" with a line through the rest of the day. Then I like those last minute invitations: "Sorry for the short notice, David, but old Joe has cried off tomorrow... could you help me out?"

"Yes please!" is my answer, unless I am already shooting.

I am ruthless about not switching shoots and, once accepted, the day's sport is inviolate, but I will drop almost any business meeting to accept a last-minute invitation to shoot. Only last season, prior acceptance of a day's shooting in Essex prevented me from accepting an invitation for a week at oryx in Namibia. Now I don't mind admitting that it was painful to pass on that!

All shooting invitations are to be highly prized. On the big days, the generosity of the host is self-evident. He is spending a lot of money to treat his guests regardless of whether his invitation is to shoot with him on his own shoot, or on a sold day on a well-known and prestigious shoot. Regular invitations to such shoots bring one within a 'charmed circle', the journalist Chapman Pinscher once said, adding that one should enjoy being part of it and bow out gracefully when eventually dropped. On bag days the lucky gun is invited into a world of privilege, in which his host entertains the guests of his choice.

Any invitations to smaller days are to be regarded by the invitee with just the same good fortune. It may be the host has a specialist shoot – some woods frequented by woodcock or, perhaps, a snipe bog. Possibly he has some pigeon shooting lined up after carefully watching flight lines for a few days. Maybe he is inviting guests to shoot over their own dogs and, on such a day, the invitee with a half co-operative spaniel may have the best day of this season or, if not, one of his special days. My old shooting friend, Ben, was once asked which the best day of his season was. He replied that he had had two. On the first he had shot in a team that took 450 fine driven pheasants. On the second, he had been one of three other guns out with me on my fen shoot, shooting over the spaniels and collecting a mixed bag of eight different species for 40 head. It may not have been true, but it was charming of him to nominate my day.

Almost all days, even poor days, have something to commend them. If, through no fault of the host, the mist and fog have stayed settled over the shoot all day then there must still be something the invited gun can find in it to enthuse about in his thank you letter. It may be a minor skirmish with some pigeons or vermin birds caught

left:
Refreshment for the guns

right:
September partridges

out by the poor visibility, or a cameo drive where, in spite of the adverse conditions, the birds flew well. Only three seasons ago, I was invited to shoot on one of the best shoots in Suffolk in just such miserable and unpromising conditions. Drawn next to a veteran farmer shot, he and I were pegged in key positions behind a belt of young trees in the first drive and experienced at least 500 French partridges flying through us at head height. Neither of us moved a muscle until, just before the end of the drive, we engaged a handful of good pheasants that got up well, unlike the partridges. That set the seal on a successful and enjoyable day in which I learned that as a very young man the farmer had shot with several of my father's associates. It was worth going just to meet him. If I am lucky, I shall one day receive a repeat invitation to that shoot and be able to see and enjoy the land over which we shot in the fog that day. Last season, I met the farmer again and was delighted to discover he recalled that drive and, like me, wondered what might have been had the day been a clear one.

My invitations have taken me shooting far and wide across the UK. Some years ago, I had an invitation from a business connection to shoot with him as his guest on Robert Jones' famous Long Mountain Shoot in Wales. My host kindly put me up overnight, and the next morning drove me to the shoot through the rain, which fortunately was clearing. Arriving at Jones'

farmhouse, with the Seven Valley below it and the mountain above, I thought it looked an awe-inspiring place to shoot, and so it was. The pheasants were high, and often gliding and curling. Only my host could make consistent sense of them, and he was assisted by cartridges, called Buffalo 4s, which I suspect are well known to high bird experts. As far as I was concerned, it was just a privilege to be there and to be a gun on this celebrated shoot. In the course of the day, I shot a few pheasants, but not very many. For the last drive of the day, Jones took us down off the mountain and placed us around a rectangular wood, much like some of the woods in my native Suffolk. I had a good stand there, shooting eight pheasants without a miss, but my host fired a box of his Buffalo 4s to little effect. Plainly, he was still allowing the lead, or giving the swing, which he had deployed so successfully against the high pheasants on the mountain. I have seen this before in a gun from Hampshire. He shot moderately all day at East Anglian birds until he engaged a single, stupendously high hen pheasant and killed it stone dead.

I also recall a distasteful incident from that day in Wales that concerned another guest of my host, who had also travelled with us from his home. Lunch was provided at the end of the day by Mr Jones in the farmhouse, and after a congenial meal, it was made known to the guns that there was an opportunity to see and thank the

above:
The author with
Midge at Snelsdon

gamekeeper for his efforts. All of us went outside to shake his hand and tip him, except for this one guest. He sat tight at the table and left without showing his appreciation in any way. My host and I were both disgusted.

Although I greatly enjoyed my Long Mountain experience, I was in no hurry to either return there or to shoot any of the other celebrated high bird shoots. This was because I didn't feel I was a good enough shot to take on such birds with any regularity, and had no wish to 'load for bear', so to speak, by acquiring a heavily choked over-and-under shotgun, through which heavily loaded cartridges could be discharged without undue recoil. I could quite understand how top class shots would wish to take on and test their skills against such tall pheasants, but I decided it was not really my game. However, if invited, I would, I suspect, happily accept and give it another go. I confess I am loath to refuse any shooting invitation.

I suppose the distinction between such shoots as Long Mountain and other shoots where there are some high bird drives, is that all the drives on Long Mountain are high bird drives unless, as were we for the last drive of the day, the guns are taken off the mountain to shoot a more moderate drive.

The variety of drives on other shoots adds great interest to a day's driven shooting, when the gun does not know how the birds will fly until the drive starts. Holker Hall, near Barrow-in-Furness, is a great example of this. Lady Grey's Bank – the invariable first drive of the day when I was shooting there – was a heavy drive with a quantity of moderate birds, and the guns did well to temper their enthusiasm if they were not to shoot the bag. I recall one gun, who really should have known better, killing one right and left after another. At the end of the drive he was reprimanded by his host. His bag filling exercise meant that the gun team would be presented with fewer high birds later in the day, when the quality drives were being tackled.

At Holker, it was well worth forbearing from shooting the moderate birds on that drive because what came later was drive after drive of quality high pheasant shooting. During 'The Cape', pheasants launched themselves off the top of a sheer cliff face and crossed the gun line in a grass field, behind which was woodland. These spectacular birds made for exquisite pheasant shooting and, years later, I can picture the scene: the guns out on the grass, the pheasants making to pass high overhead, often curling as they did so, and the sound of shots under the pale, wintry sky.

In another drive I was a walking gun, out on the flank of a kale game cover – it was too northerly for maize – and I remember overlooking the gun line far below and spotting the bald pate of one of the guns who

above:
Braced in the game cart

was shooting hatless. The birds that flew forward from that block of kale appeared to be out of shot of the guns, but I did not have time to worry about that for long. As pheasants started to break out on my flank, I heard the keeper shout, "Cut them down, sir!" and I got to work with my gun.

On another drive, the high numbered guns stood in a ride way cut though woodland, number one at the top and numbers two, three, four and five lower down the slope. The quality of the shooting improved with the distance the gun was pegged downhill, but numbers six, seven and eight had the prime spots. They were not in the woodland at all, but stood in marram grass on the edge of the sea shore. There, the pheasants were curling across a small bay and were, at times, literally over the sea. These were unique stands. Having had a peg in the ride on the first occasion I shot the drive, I was lucky enough to be on the beach another time. I had some superb shooting in these unusual surroundings.

Even with all these excellent drives there was a drive that everyone wanted to shoot at Holker Hall, and that was called The Reak. There the guns lined a gully with a woody bank in front of them, at the top of which were tall, mature hardwood trees. I believe that behind these trees there was a game cover. I say 'believe', because I never saw it. The drive started with some beaters tapping the bank uphill away from the guns, and the height of these chaps above the

watching guns was awesome in itself. It was a long way up to the top of the bank. When they had climbed to the top, they faded out and the drive started with the early birds flying over the high number guns at the left-hand end of the line. Gradually, the pheasants became more widespread and there was action all along the line.

I recall quite clearly how, as a gun, I saw the pheasants flying over the tall trees, and then how they invariably set their wings and started to drop as they came on over the trees on the bank and the gun line. Tall, dropping on set wings and often curling, they were awesome. In a survey of top shots in Edwardian England nine out of 10 guns rated such pheasants as the most difficult shots, so in finding them difficult we were in historic company. On one of these drives I hit a purple patch and accounted for half a dozen. It made me feel as if I was Ripon or Waslingham himself.

Recently, I met a gun who had shot with me there – he was someone I had not seen for years – and after greeting me he smiled at the recollection of "those birds over the beach," and, "those incredible pheasants from the Reak!"

The shooting host who invites guests to shoot far away from home is to be applauded as particularly generous. He has not only to provide the shooting, but also organise, if not actually pay for, the accommodation for his guests and their partners, and for the food and drink they consume. He also has to handle a miscellaneous range of problems before they can settle down comfortably. One important guest insists on his beloved gundog sleeping on, or perhaps even in, his bed in a 'no dog' lodge. The lodge management team must one way or another be persuaded to turn a blind eye. Another only drinks 'Black Balls' whisky. Special supplies have to be ordered and delivered. A third guest has a wife accompanying him who is allergic to almost everything, and arranging to feed her is a nightmare for the poor host.

Some years ago, I was lucky enough to be asked to shoot in the Braes of Angus where we, as a team, stayed in a fine lodge there which made for a good social side to the shooting party. As in all such parties, there was a varied mix of guns from different backgrounds. There were the farmers, who were at the grouse throughout the autumn and then turned to the partridges, before devoting their winters to the relentless pursuit of the pheasant. Then there were business types, whose time for shooting was limited. 'The farmers' usually owned and used inherited family guns. They shot with understated, elegant, practised skill. The entrepreneurs used continental over-and-under shotguns and shot the pheasants as if they were clay targets.

Although there were one or two indifferent 'doggerel' drives, which were doomed to produce low, forgettable pheasants, most of the drives were shooting sonnets. On my first morning, I was placed on the forward face of a steep bank rising from the River Prosen. Surrounded by silver birch and the woodland so typical of the north east of Scotland, there was a clearing in front of me and clear sky above. My task was to kill the pheasants in this hole in the woods. I accounted for five or six, all inviting, challenging shots, which was made doubly pleasurable by the beauty of the surroundings and particularly the rocky river below.

Several of these wonderful drives involved the guns standing on one side of the river and the beaters making good the cover on the other. Later on, we were to stand on the river bank, with the river now in front of us, as the game lifted from high ground opposite and flew back over us. Here and there were swales, which went away up the hill before disappearing into the grouse moor above. Hardy kale had been planted and protected in this marginal ground, and even hardier pheasants were fed up to these strategic points. The pheasants, making for the safety of the low ground on shoot days, had a natural start on any bird getting airborne in Suffolk, and even the low ones were high birds there.

Looking back several years, I repeat in a sincere way those well-worn words of the lucky guest gun, "Thanks so much!"

And then, I ask, how you can ever thank a shooting host who has given you such fine sport? The answer to that is you write him a thank you letter. I notice with rather crusty regret that more and more shooting thank you letters come by e-mail – a rag-tag postillion for such an important missive. Nothing less than a hand written letter sent by snail mail meets the needs, and the best of them are veritable works of art, sonnets in praise of game shooting. Thankfully, I cannot quote from any of my own as I never keep copies, and was likely so tired after the day's shooting that I could not remember what I wrote. However, I have files filled with the letters penned by my guests. I appreciate them all, and many relate to days spent on my fen shoot Lark Hall Farm.

Looking back though the old files in which I keep them, I have come across one from a 12-year-old who had shot his first duck with me that particular day, and had also wiped his father's eye, by shooting an easy cock pheasant. "A day I will remember for a long time," he wrote, and I bet he will. The script has the usual schoolboy's errors and would have taken him a painful, tortured hour to write. But he wrote it and posted it and he'll get another invitation.

The Colonel's letters laid proper emphasis on the 'hunting' aspect of the day and the fun had by the spaniels and the guns, even if not always at the same time. When a Lark Hall day has been particularly energetic, as some of them can be, then the Colonel sometimes confesses to having had a couple of large glasses of whisky during the evening afterwards.

In rooting through my file, I found another letter, which opened with the excellent line: "Having tipped the good bottle severely, am lying in a scalding bath... memories of the towering, high, wild fen pheasants in the unforgiving sky..." Alas, poor Peacock, he's left us now.

Sometimes I think the British Armed Services are the last bastions of good manners in a manner-less country, and their officers invariably write good thank you letters. One, from the officer's mess at Honington, contains a delightful apology for "spoiling the first drive". He had, too. Tasked to walk in line across a field to a dyke with the purpose of jumping the duck (if there were any) on it, he had put up and engaged a hare 100 yards short of the dyke. It got worse for him as on the way home his Labrador, lying in the back of the truck, had quietly consumed one of the few pheasants we had shot during the day. Other courteous and appreciative notes from messes up and down the country recall memories of fun days in the field.

In the thank you letters of my oldest friends, mention is not infrequently made of the dubious character of my other guests, their fellow guns on the day. Old Ben wrote to me after one day describing them as "a rough a crew as one could wish to be out with..." and looking at the names of the other guns that day I must say he was right. In an earlier letter he had touched on this same topic: "You always have such a good crew to shoot and a diverse one as well – the young bucks and the old dogs."

The most scurrilous of these letter writers are acute observers of the day, and as host I have learnt much from them about my own shoot, my guests, and the events of the day, some of which others would rather were concealed from me. One I have here from Agriman opens with a tirade of criticism about the shortcomings of the other guns' dogs (he had no dog of his own). He found he could express pleasure at meeting the 'new' gun, whose dog he described nicely as "even smaller but more use than Trembler's rat".

Another small and less extreme shoot, in which I was involved for a while, has left me with an amusing file of thank you letters. Inevitably, some of the same writers feature with thank you letters relating to

below:
Good company

their experiences here. A brief, enthusiastic card from the Trembler referred to above is among the exhibits. The front of this card pictures a red-faced gun in his bath with a tumbler of scotch. The manuscript commends the day and infers some success with the dog – 'the rat' – and with the gun, although I know from other sources that Trembler had been eye wiped in humiliating circumstances by Agriman. Word of this would already have spread all over Trembler's home county and the pressure would be mounting on him to up his game and improve his accuracy as the season progressed.

Other amusing contributions come from a pal who makes beer. Reflecting on one of the days, he refers to arriving in the yard to find me trying to unlock the barn door assisted by "a team of well-seasoned beaters." I liked that as that beating team (that word is a misnomer if ever there was one) had an average age on the high side of 80. In another letter, a reference to how he had revelled in the view of my laying out the tablecloths shows how a shoot host can never be too careful. He's under observation all the time, and there is a danger on a small shoot like ours that he may provide the guests with more entertainment than the game.

Having hosted many other days over the years, ranging from the roughest by days to full-scale driven shoots, and in different parts of the country, I have yet another file with thank you letters from these. I note that some of the same names crop up more often than others, and that makes me think my invitation list was either restricted by those few guns who would shoot with me or, if I am in a more charitable mode, the fact that these were the mates I enjoyed shooting with down the years. One gun – the beer maker as it happens – shot with me on several different shoots but, for some inexplicable reason, never got into the shooting to any extent at all. Eventually, I took him to shoot partridges on a full-scale, proper partridge shoot in north-west Norfolk only for him to experience yet another thin day. In the following year, I took him to the same shoot and once again he was out of the shooting. I was mortified that so much expenditure and planning on my part should have been frustrated by him having another bad draw that reduced him to a virtual spectator for most of the day. In hindsight, I can see the funny side of it, assisted by a carefully crafted letter from the beer maker, written in the depth of that sense of injustice and misery that afflicts even the most relaxed and charitable guns when they have missed out on the shooting all day. Nicely described by him as the rudest shooting thank you letter he had ever written, he suggested that I may have been in doubt as to whether I was inviting him to shoot or to watch me shooting. If it was, he added, the message was well embedded. He went on to suggest the

keeper must have been bribed to drive the game over 'Father and Son Barnes', whose ruthless shooting policy he also elaborated on in some detail. He said that in travelling home with another gun, an occasional guest of mine, they had discussed our respective "kills, bludgeonings and maimings" and then set to work out the percentage of the bag we had accounted for between us, with their estimates varying between 35 and 70 per cent. This ill-informed speculation was all embittered rambling of a brewer, but made for good reading at my end and has given me occasional amusement ever since.

I am always amused to revisit the letters I receive from a certain well-known Norfolk farmer, ever the shooting enthusiast and always armed with a decent dog in addition to his gun. I never fail to glean from him an account of his champagne moments during a day, such as when he describes a drive on which "there were birds everywhere but managed to score a couple of long, low scudders to my right… and then the curse of missing the last pheasant of the season."

I saw him at work on the right flank of that drive, out on his own on the edge of the rushes, and his description brings the scene all back to me.

All these letters, received and filed over all too many years, highlight the fun my friends have had shooting with me, and I like to think I have given as much pleasure and amusement as I have received in shooting.

The Spent Cartridge

By the time we returned home after shooting one day at Lark Hall Farm, it was long dark. We divided the chores between us; one was to hang the game in the game larder, another to feed the dogs, and a third to get in the guns and kit. For a few minutes there was much to do, and it seemed like there was more to do than there was because we were all tired after the exercise, excitement and fresh air of the day's sport. Then, once these tasks had been completed, we moved to a room in the heart of the home to clean the guns.

Companionably, we revisited the incidents of the day. We touched on routine occurrences, how we had found nothing at home in the North Dyke, and how we had bolted a rabbit from the river bank that had escaped. As Simon's futile double-barrelled effort had been made in front of us all, this was still the cause of considerable amusement. We made a count of the duck shot per gun off the Pumping Station Drain.

While we talked, I put a bottle of whisky, a jug and tumblers on the sideboard, there for anyone who wanted a whisky. I had one and the first taste and effect of it was perfect, as it always is after a winter day spent rough shooting. We talked and drank quietly and slowly, and worked on our guns. My old Webley & Scott 12-bore was in three pieces on the table. I have shot with this old gun since I was 18 years old. It's not a smart gun, but it's mine: a present from my father, it came from the great gun shop, Gallyons of Cambridge, so its very provenance is

right:
spent cartridges

redolent with my own early life. I picked up the stock, heavily cast on for my strong left eye and, in doing that, was reminded of the impact Andrew Perkins had on my shooting, when I took my guns to him at his shooting school. I still hear his question ringing in my ears: "Do you shoot like a prat, Mr Barnes?" even before he had seen me fire a shot.

I looked at the stock again and noticed a small bruise on the right-hand side, the result of a careless encounter with the sharp edge of a ferret box. I made a mental note to get Perry, my gunsmith, to give that some attention. The forend is pinned and, routinely, I check it is not showing any sign of splitting again. It did split once, back in the 1970s when I believe Eley had its famous Grand Prix cartridges loaded in Eastern Europe, with the resultant version of that then-popular cartridge being sharper than it should have been. I finished oiling the mechanical parts and put it down before picking up the barrels. As I did so, my hand snagged momentarily on the rib, where there is a rough, jagged place. That was caused by two male Labradors when I was shooting in Sutherland two seasons back. I fast tracked back to the hillside underneath the wild, wind-blown wood where that incident occurred. The keeper and I were looking for birds at the end of the drive and had leaned our unloaded guns on a large, smooth, oval rock. Suddenly we had heard a commotion, and these two dogs were at each other's throats in a short battle, in the course of which they knocked our two guns together and damaged both of them. As we ruefully inspected the damage to our respective shotguns, the keeper remarked on the injustice of it. These two dogs had had a choice of 70,000 acres of Sutherland in which to fight, and had chosen the rock against which our guns were resting. There's another job for the gunsmith there, I thought, as I gave the barrels a vigorous clean.

When that job was done, we tidied away cartridge bags and belts and locked up the guns. By then, I was hoping there might be a bath to be had and, with the post shooting day glow well on now, ambled off for a soak. When I came down, I went in to check the spaniels. I found them together in their box. They had been brought back from the shoot in their dog bags, and by now my old chap, Brandy, had wriggled out of his and was lying full length on the floor of the box. The little sprocker bitch was still rugged up and raised her eyes, but not her head, on my approach. Brandy thumped his tail without moving and I could see from the movement of the bag that the little sprocker's rudder was gently acknowledging me.

I looked at these two beautiful animals and then knelt down by their box to stroke them both. As I held the head of my old dog, I thought back to the hunting he had done during the day when he had been at work in the reeds. I had one cameo of him emerging from the reed bed with a

lively mallard drake in his mouth, plodding purposefully towards me over the mud. In another, he was hunting hard on the line of a cock pheasant running on towards the far end of a long dyke. I was watching him working out the line, in and out of the steep dyke, first one side and then the other. It was a hunt he had had 100 times before; a hunt at which he was an expert. There were two heading guns, half concealed in cover, and my companion and I making towards them reducing the distance and the odds all the time. At last, after fossicking more intently than ever in the bottom of the dyke, Brandy flushed his pheasant, which as a last resort used his wings and sought to escape in a fast,

low scud to the left of the heading guns. One of them dropped it and Brandy retrieved, bringing the game to hand.

So, as I cradled his old head, my feelings were of overwhelming affection. Yes, in name I had handled and shot over this great working springer spaniel all day, but in truth he had handled himself. We had shot together as master and dog but also, after the years of sport we had shared, as companions. The old dog could not understand my words of pleasure and gratitude, but my affection was gratefully received. These dogs were hurting, as they rested after the exertions of the day. They looked at me as if to say, we will do anything for you other than move.

As I regarded the old dog, I reflected on the brevity of a shooting dog's life and the cruel way in which such beloved companions have to leave their owners so soon. Then, more positively, I thought about how with a night's sleep and a day's rest he would be ready to work again. Old bones and aching muscles would ease up again after a little time and enable him to hunt. My next appearance in shooting clothes would make him delirious with delight and with a desire to work in the woods and fields. I knew that so long as he was at home no shoot day could ever be greeted by me with anything less than enthusiasm.

Apart from a spaniel at work there is nothing I like to watch more than a spaniel in resting mode. By now the little bitch had worked herself round in front of the old dog, so that he was comfortably curled round her. I gave them a biscuit each and crept away. Elsewhere in the house I could hear the cheerful party sounds that precede a shooting day supper. The sitting room was full to overflowing with relaxed and contented men and women. The talk was generally on the subject of the day's shoot, other shoots and shooting. The drinks fizzed in the flutes. This was a champagne moment.

And then to supper, and to my last task of the day: to carve the venison. I take it as no insult when my nephews disrespectfully refer to me as "Our eat-what-he-kills uncle." I knew the provenance of this particular

tender fallow saddle. It happened that one winter evening I descended from my high seat when it was really too dark to shoot, and, while standing at the bottom of it, realised a deer had come out of the wood 80 yards along. I could make it out with my binoculars and it was broadside on, looking towards me. Taking a lean off the ladder of my high seat, I looked thought the scope. It was getting dark, really dark, and the 'picture' wasn't clear. I shouldn't have shot, but on the other hand a shot at a fallow doe was so rare that I was tempted. Aiming as best I could, I squeezed the trigger and thought I saw the deer wobble before it made off up the face of the wood and then disappeared into it. I followed up with a small head torch, and made out the animal lying just inside the wood. She had expired there and there was no need for another shot. Unloading the rifle, I had soon fixed a drag rope to the beast and pulled it out of the wood in readiness for recovery to the deer larder. A late finish that night made the taste of venison all the sweeter on the night of that shoot party.

The saddle of this doe was on the table and, with recollections of the evening on which I collected it bright in my mind, I carved succulent pink slices of venison. The plates around the table filled up with the meat and vegetables: fen onions and potatoes from the farm on which we had been shooting, green vegetables from the local allotment expert, redcurrant jelly from my garden. There was no sign of nouvelle cuisine, and the only thing French item on the table was the claret in the decanters. And that's how I liked it: a simple English supper at the end of an English shooting day.

Over many years I have been privileged to enjoy so many wonderful shoot lunches and suppers, each unique to the host and hostess who provide it. Lunch with old Bob always featured port likely to delight seasoned connoisseurs, as privileged guests sipped some rarely-seen vintage, often unawares.

Lunch with the young Colonel was invariably bangers and mash. It had been good enough for the old Colonel, so was good enough for him! The Colonel's shoot was a proper rough shooting day, a hunt more than a shoot, often quite literally as the whipper-in of the local pack would likely put in an appearance with a truck full of hunt terriers. Thrashing through the undergrowth was hard work, and so the bangers and mash were just right for lunch for a team with an appetite. As to the thirst, the young Colonel looked after that too.

Rookery Farm shoot lunches followed a time-honoured path. After shooting, the bag was counted, sweep winner announced, the keeper tipped and goodbyes said to the beaters, all in the yard. The guns would then drift house-wards for a cup of tea or, if house guests, the quickest of hot baths and a change of clothes. Then a gin and tonic

preceded a warm by the fire, before lunch at five. And what a lunch! The Rookery lady hit the spot time and time again with delicious, gourmet-standard starters, main courses and puddings. Fine wines were not excluded from the proceedings either. These evening meals were most congenial and amusing, and a fitting conclusion to the wonderful days' shooting given to the guest guns there. Invariably it was late in the evening before wives and daughters of the various local guns would put their heads round the dining room door as they attempted to extract their often tired and emotional husbands or fathers.

I liked those long evening meals after shooting when, with the companions of the day, I could enjoy good food and wine and conversation. I was, however, just as happy to sit down with my boots on in a barn and get through lunch at a brisk pace so that the guns could return to the field for a really good, long afternoon's sport. Hot or cold, such a lunch has more the sense of a break in the serious business of the day, and there is no place in it for starters and puddings or for the use of (much) alcohol. On my rough shoots, the picnic took some planning and organisation because of the distance from home and the absence of facilities. Nevertheless, some good, convivial lunch breaks were spent in the farm's one shed. Even less elaborate were the days I spent engaged in highland rough shooting, when a piece in the game bag or

the poacher's pocket would have to suffice, with a drink from the burn to slake the thirst. No matter what the lunch was or what form it took, when eaten with good shooting friends and companions, it was an important part of the fabric of the day.

In season, thoughts of shooting were never far from my mind. When dressing in the morning, the glimpse of my shooting suit in the wardrobe or a pair of freshly washed shooting stockings would set me off. I liked the rough feel of good tweed, its colour and its smell. I never felt happier than when I was dressing in my plus four suit in the pre-dawn light of a winter morning before driving to some distant shoot.

Downstairs, I would carry a couple of leather cartridge bags to the truck and my gun in its canvas slip. All the kit was always prepared and made ready the previous night. This was not just kit, it was my kit, cherished for years and often many times repaired. It all went towards my enjoyment of the shooting day.

Shooting sport was – and is – no trivial, ephemeral thing for me. It was no mere ball game. It was in the heart of me. It made my heyday. And now, as I look back, I have no regrets of the many happy days I have spent with dog and gun, and I still greet and treat each shooting day as if it is my last. My youthful enthusiasm is undiminished, and only rarely do I sense the shadows lengthen as, after firing my last shot of the day, I eject the spent cartridge.

Acknowledgements

I am obliged to Peter Carr for writing the foreword, and for his editorial encouragement. I am also indebted to his sub-editor, Nicola Turner, for her good-humoured assistance with the publication of this book.

I wish to thank my colleague, Theresa Gibbs, for her IT skill and other input, which she has patiently and kindly provided. John Thornley, OBE, has once again helped and encouraged me, and has endorsed the back cover with a generous recommendation.

Many of the images have been most kindly provided by friends, friends of friends and associates in the shooting world. These include Ben Blackett-Orde, Richard Clarke, Ben French, Erich and Sue Maser, Jason and Rachel Simpson, Peter Spence, Ben Stanton, John Thornley, William Walker-Arnott, Alan Waugh and Charles Willoughby. I would like to thank all of them for the considerable trouble they have taken to help me with these.

In Search of Supper is reproduced by kind permission of Sally Mitchell Fine Arts Ltd. on the cover of this book.

I wish to thank all these persons for their assistance, but any errors or defects are mine.